Gaming

Electronic Mediations

Katherine Hayles, Mark Poster, and Samuel Weber, Series Editors

Gaming

Essays on Algorithmic Culture

Alexander R. Galloway

Electronic Mediations, Volume 18

University of Minnesota Press
Minneapolis
London

Chapter 3 was originally published as "Social Realism in Gaming," *Game Studies* 4, no. 1 (November 2004). Chapter 4 was originally published as "Playing the Code: Allegories of Control in *Civilization*," *Radical Philosophy* 128 (November–December 2004). Reprinted with permission.

Published by the University of Minnesota Press
111 Third Avenue South, Suite 290
Minneapolis, MN 55401-2520
http://www.upress.umn.edu

Library of Congress Cataloging-in-Publication Data

Galloway, Alexander R., 1974–
    Gaming : essays on algorithmic culture / Alexander R. Galloway.
        p.   cm. — (Electronic mediations)
    Includes bibliographical references and index.
    ISBN-13: 978-0-8166-4850-4 (hc : alk. paper)
    ISBN-10: 0-8166-4850-6 (hc : alk. paper)
    ISBN-13: 978-0-8166-4851-1 (pb : alk. paper)
    ISBN-10: 0-8166-4851-4 (pb : alk. paper)
    1. Video games—Social aspects.   2. Video games—Philosophy.
I. Title.   II. Series.
    GV1469.34.S63G35   2006
    794.8—dc22   2006003428

Printed in the United States of America on acid-free paper

The University of Minnesota is an equal-opportunity educator and employer.

12 11 10 09 08 07 06   10 9 8 7 6 5 4 3 2 1

For Munro

Representation no longer exists;
there's only action.

—*Gilles Deleuze*
"Intellectuals and Power"

The new media are oriented towards
action, not contemplation; towards the
present, not tradition.

—*Hans Magnus Enzensberger*
"Constituents of a Theory
of the Media"

Contents

Preface

Philosophy, Gilles Deleuze and Félix Guattari wrote late in life, is about the creation of concepts. To them a concept is always a type of vector for thought, a cognitive vehicle designed to move things from one place to another. In the five essays in this book, I try to formulate a few conceptual movements, a few conceptual algorithms, for thinking about video games. What is an algorithm if not a machine for the motion of parts? And it is the artfulness of the motion that matters most. Following Deleuze and Guattari, I wish my conceptual algorithms to be as ad hoc, as provisional, as cobbled together as theirs were. Let them be what Northrop Frye once called "an interconnected group of suggestions."

Video games have been central to mass culture for more than twenty years, yet surprisingly few books today attempt a critical analysis of the medium. In this study, I try not to reduce video game studies to other fields, such as literary criticism or cinema studies, nor do I attempt to dissect games as mere data for sociological or anthropological research. Instead, I attempt an analysis of what Fredric Jameson calls "the poetics of social forms," that is, the aesthetic and political impact of video games as a formal medium.

So, at the end of the day, this book is not a book about video games, just as Jameson's *Signatures of the Visible* is not a book about film in any narrow sense. The text by Jameson offers instead certain conceptual algorithms for modernity, the information age, and the various aesthetic and political realities at play within them. I hope that my book will approximate something similar.

"No more vapor theory anymore," wrote Geert Lovink. This applies to the video game generation as much as anyone else. Our generation needs to shrug off the contributions of those who view this as all so new and shocking. They came from somewhere else and are still slightly unnerved by digital technology. We were born here and love it. Short attention spans, cultural fragmentation, the speeding up of life, identifying change in every nook and cranny—these are neuroses in the imagination of the doctor, not the life of the patient. So, above all, this book is about loving video games. It's about exploring their artistry, their political possibility, their uniqueness. The first question is: Do you play video games? Then next we may explore what they do.

Acknowledgments

I am grateful to the following for inspiration and assistance on this book: Cory Arcangel, Joline Blais, Brody Condon, Mark Daggett, Mary Flanagan, Jane Gaines, Munro Galloway, Jon Ippolito, Paul Johnson, Steven Johnson, Susan Murray, David Parisi, Katie Salen, Anne-Marie Schleiner, Eddo Stern, Eugene Thacker, Mark Van de Walle, and McKenzie Wark. My graduate seminar at New York University in spring 2005 provided invaluable feedback on the manuscript. Writing and gameplay for this book occurred primarily during the years 1999 through 2005, bookended by the games *Half-Life* and *World of Warcraft*.

1

Gamic Action, Four Moments

A game is an activity defined by rules in which players try to reach some sort of goal. Games can be whimsical and playful, or highly serious. They can be played alone or in complex social scenarios. This book, however, is not about games in the abstract, nor is it about games of all varieties, electronic or not. There is little here on game design, or performance, or imaginary worlds, or nonlinear narrative. I avoid any extended reflection on the concept of play. Rather, this book starts and ends with a specific mass medium, the medium of the video game from the 1970s to the beginning of the new millennium. A few detours will be necessary along the way: to the cinema, and to the computer.

A video game is a cultural object, bound by history and materiality, consisting of an electronic computational device and a game simulated in software. The electronic computational device—the machine, for short—may come in a variety of forms. It may be a personal computer, an arcade machine, a home console, a portable device, or any number of other electronic machines.[1] The machine will typically have some sort of input device, such as a keyboard or controller, and also have some sort of intelligible surface for output such as a screen or other physical interface. Loaded into the machine's storage is the game software. Software is data; the data issue instructions to the hardware of the machine, which in turn executes those instructions on the physical level by moving bits of information from one place to another, performing logical operations on other data, triggering physical devices, and so on. The software instructs the machine to simulate the rules of the game through meaningful action. The player, or operator,[2] is an individual agent who communicates with the software and hardware of the machine, sending codified messages via input devices and receiving codified messages via output devices. Taking these elements in sum, I use the term "gaming" to refer to the entire apparatus of the video game. It is a massive cultural medium involving large numbers of organic machines and inorganic machines. Embedded as it is in the information systems of the millenary society, this medium will likely remain significant for some time to come.

Begin like this: If photographs are images, and films are moving images, then *video games are actions*. Let this be word one for video game theory. Without action, games remain only in the pages of an abstract rule book. Without the active participation of players and machines, video games exist only as static computer code. Video games come into being when the machine is powered up and the software is executed; they exist when enacted.

Video games are actions. Consider the formal differences between video games and other media: indeed, one *takes* a photograph, one *acts* in a film. But these actions transpire before or during the fabrication of the work, a work that ultimately assumes the form of a physical object (the print). With video games, the work itself is material action. One *plays* a game. And the software *runs*. The operator and the machine play the video game together, step by step, move by move. Here the "work" is not as solid or integral as in other media. Consider the difference between camera and joystick, or between image and action, or between watching and doing. In his work on the cinema, Gilles Deleuze used the term "action-image" to describe the expression of force or action in film. With video games, the action-image has survived but now exists not as a particular historical or formal instance of representation but as the base foundation of an entirely

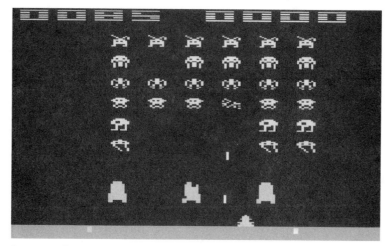

Space Invaders, Taito Corporation, 1978

new medium. "Games are both object and process," writes Espen Aarseth, "they can't be read as texts or listened to as music, they must be played."[3] To understand video games, then, one needs to understand how action exists in gameplay, with special attention to its many variations and intensities.

One should resist equating gamic action with a theory of "interactivity" or the "active audience" theory of media. Active audience theory claims that audiences always bring their own interpretations and receptions of the work. Instead I embrace the claim, rooted in cybernetics and information technology, that an active medium is one whose very materiality moves and restructures itself—pixels turning on and off, bits shifting in hardware registers, disks spinning up and spinning down. Because of this potential confusion, I avoid the word "interactive" and prefer instead to call the video game, like the computer, an *action-based* medium.[4]

Because of this, for the first time in a long time there comes an interesting upheaval in the area of mass culture. What used to be primarily the domain of eyes and looking is now more likely that of muscles and doing, *thumbs*, to be sure, and what used to be the act of reading is now the act of doing, or just "the act." In other words, while the mass media of film, literature, television, and so on continue to

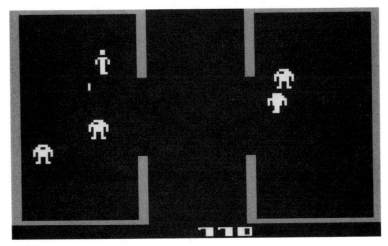

Berzerk, Stern Electronics, 1980

engage in various debates around representation, textuality, and subjectivity, there has emerged in recent years a whole new medium,
computers and in particular video games, whose foundation is not in
looking and reading but in the instigation of material change through
action. And the most curious part of the upheaval is, to borrow what
Critical Art Ensemble said once about hackers, that the most important cultural workers today are children.

People move their hands, bodies, eyes, and mouths when they
play video games. But machines also act. They act in response to
player actions as well as independently of them. Philip Agre uses the
phrase "grammars of action" to describe how human activities are
coded for machinic parsing using linguistic and structural metaphors.[5]
Video games create their own grammars of action; the game controller
provides the primary physical vocabularies for humans to pantomime
these gestural grammars. But beyond the controller, games also have
their own grammars of action that emerge through gameplay. These
grammars are part of the code. They help pass messages from object
to object inside the machine's software. But they also help to articu-
late higher-level actions, actions experienced in common game oc-
currences such as power-ups or network lag.

One may start by distinguishing two basic types of action in video games: machine actions and operator actions. The difference is this: machine actions are acts performed by the software and hardware of the game computer, while operator actions are acts performed by players. So, winning *Metroid Prime* is the operator's act, but losing it is the machine's. Locating a power-up in *Super Mario Bros.* is an operator act, but the power-up actually boosting the player character's health is a machine act.

Of course, the division is completely artificial—both the machine and the operator work together in a cybernetic relationship to effect the various actions of the video game in its entirety. The two types of action are ontologically the same. In fact, in much of gameplay, the two actions exist as a *unified, single phenomenon*, even if they are distinguishable for the purposes of analysis. This book will not privilege one type of action over the other (as analyses of other media often do)—in video games the action of the machine is just as important as the action of the operator.

But, you may ask, where is the fun in a game played by an "operator" and a "machine"? Video games can be intensely fun. They immerse and enthrall. Time-wise, video games garner significant investment by players. This happens in gaming to an extent not seen in other mass media. Many games are rated at sixty or eighty hours of total gameplay; some, like *Sims Online* or *World of Warcraft*, far exceed that. But a video game is not simply a fun toy. It is also an algorithmic machine and like all machines functions through specific, codified rules of operation. The player—the "operator"—is the one who must engage with this machine. In our day and age, this is the site of fun. It is also the work site. I adopt the terms "operator" and "machine" not to diminish the value of fun, meaningful play but to stress that in the sphere of electronic media, games are fundamentally cybernetic software systems involving both organic and nonorganic actors.

As the great German media theorist Friedrich Kittler wrote, code is the only language that does what it says. Code is not only a syntactic and semantic language; it is also a machinic language. At runtime, code moves. Code effects physical change in a very literal sense. Logic gates open and close. Electrons flow. Display devices illuminate. Input

Warcraft III, Blizzard Entertainment, 2002

devices and storage devices transubstantiate between the physical and the mathematical. Video games are games, yes, but more importantly they are software systems; this must always remain in the forefront of one's analysis. In blunt terms, the video game *Dope Wars* has more in common with the finance software *Quicken* than it does with traditional games like chess, roulette, or billiards. Thus it is from the perspective of informatic software, of *algorithmic cultural objects*, that this book unfolds.

Gamic action is customarily described as occurring within a separate, semiautonomous space that is removed from normal life. The French sociologist and anthropologist Roger Caillois writes that games are "make-believe," that they are "accompanied by a special awareness of a second reality or of a free unreality, as against real life."[6] The Dutch cultural historian Johan Huizinga agrees, writing that play transpires "quite consciously outside 'ordinary' life."[7]

   Thus in addition to the previous split between machine and operator, a second analytical distinction is possible: in video games there are actions that occur in diegetic space and actions that occur in

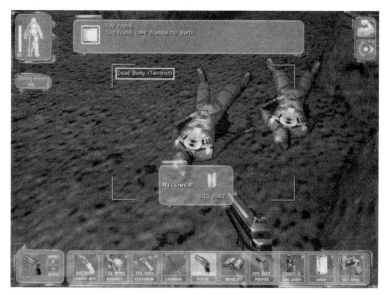

Deus Ex, Ion Storm, 2000

nondiegetic space. I adopt the terms "diegetic" and "nondiegetic" from literary and film theory. But in the migration from one medium to another, the meaning of the terms will no doubt change slightly.[8] The diegesis of a video game is the game's total world of narrative action. As with cinema, video game diegesis includes both onscreen and offscreen elements. It includes characters and events that are shown, but also those that are merely made reference to or are presumed to exist within the game situation. While some games may not have elaborate narratives, there always exists some sort of elementary play scenario or play situation—Caillois's "second reality"— which functions as the diegesis of the game. In *PONG* it is a table, a ball, and two paddles; in *World of Warcraft* it is two large continents with a sea in between. By contrast, nondiegetic play elements are those elements of the gaming apparatus that are external to the world of narrative action. In film theory, "nondiegetic" refers to a whole series of formal techniques that are part of the apparatus of the film while still outside the narrative world of the film, such as a film's score or titles. With "nondiegetic" I wish to evoke this same terrain for video games: gamic elements that are inside the total gamic apparatus yet ortion of the apparatus that constitutes a pretend world and story. To be sure, nondiegetic elements are often ...rally connected to the act of gameplay, so being nondiegetic does not necessarily mean being nongamic. Sometimes nondiegetic elements are firmly embedded in the game world. Sometimes they are entirely removed. The heads-up display (HUD) in *Deus Ex* is nondiegetic, while the various rooms and environments in the game are diegetic. Or in *Berzerk*, pressing Start is a nondiegetic act, whereas shooting robots is a diegetic act. Likewise, activating the Pause button in *Max Payne* is a nondiegetic act, but activating the slow-motion effect during a gunfight is a diegetic act. As will become evident, the nondiegetic is much more common in gaming than in film or literature, and likewise it will be much more central to my study. In fact, I find that the need to employ the concept of the diegetic at all stems not from a desire to reduce games to narrative texts, but quite the opposite: since the nondiegetic is so important in video games, it is impossible not to employ the concept, even in a negative issuance. And indeed, in some instances it will be difficult to demarcate the difference between diegetic and nondiegetic acts in a video game, for the process of good game continuity is to fuse these acts together as seamlessly as possible.

The superimposition of these two orthogonal axes—machine and operator, diegetic and nondiegetic—is a deliberate attempt to embrace a broad theory of gamic action.[9] I wish to make room here for the entire medium of the video game. In this model, pressing Pause is as significant as shooting a weapon. Cheats are as significant as strategies. Other approaches might miss this. The four quadrants of these two axes will provide the structure for the rest of the chapter. Thus I offer here four moments of gamic action. Each will uncover a different perspective on the formal qualities of the video game.

Pure Process

The first quadrant is about the machinic phylum and the vitality of pure matter. Consider Yu Suzuki's *Shenmue*. One plays *Shenmue* by participating in its *process*. Remove everything and there is still action, a gently stirring rhythm of life. There is a privileging of the quotidian,

Shenmue, Sega AM2, 2000

the simple. As in the films of Yasujiro Ozu, the experience of time is important. There is a repetition of movement and dialogue ("On that day the snow changed to rain," the characters repeat). One step leads slowly and deliberately to the next. There is a slow, purposeful accumulation of experiences. When games like *Shenmue* are left alone, they often settle into a moment of equilibrium. Not a tape loop, or a skipped groove, but a state of rest. The game is slowly walking in place, shifting from side to side and back again to the center. It is running, playing itself, perhaps. The game is in an ambient state, an *ambience act*. Not all games have this action, but when they do, they can exist in an ambience act indefinitely. No significant stimulus from the game environment will disturb the player character. *Grand Theft Auto III* defaults to the ambience act. Almost all moments of gameplay in *Final Fantasy X* can momentarily revert to an ambience act if the gamer simply stops playing and walks away. *Shenmue*, despite its clock, reverts to the ambience act. Things continue to change when caught in an ambience act, but nothing changes that is of any importance. No stopwatch runs down. No scores are lost. If the passage of time means anything at all, then the game is not in an ambient state. It rains. The sun goes down, then it comes up. Trees stir. These acts are a type of perpetual happening, a living tableau. Ambience acts are distinguishable from a game pause through the existence of micromovements—just like the small, visible movements described by Deleuze as the "affect-image." They signal that the game is still under way, but that no gameplay is actually happening at the moment. The game is still present, but play is absent. Micromovements often come in the form of pseudorandom repetitions of rote gamic action, or ordered collections of repetitions that cycle with different periodicities to add complexity to the ambience act. The machine is still *on* in an ambience act, but the operator is away. Gameplay recommences as soon as the operator returns with controller input. The ambience act is the machine's act. The user is on hold, but the machine keeps on working. In this sense, an ambience act is the inverse of pressing Pause. While the *machine* pauses in a pause act and the operator is free to take a break, it is the *operator* who is paused in an ambience act, leaving the machine to hover in a state of pure process.

The ambience act is an action executed by the machine and thus emanates outward to the operator (assuming that he or she has stuck around to witness it). In this sense, it follows the logic of the traditionally expressive or representational forms of art such as painting or film. The world of the game exists as a purely aesthetic object in the ambience act. It can be looked at; it is detached from the world, a self-contained expression. But there is always a kind of "charged expectation" in the ambience act.[10] It is about possibility, a subtle solicitation for the operator to return.

Likewise there is another category related to the ambience act that should be described in slightly inverted terms. These are the various interludes, segues, and other machinima that constitute the purely cinematic segments of a game. James Newman uses the term "off-line" to describe these moments of player passivity, as opposed to the "on-line" moments of actual gameplay.[11] Most video games incorporate time-based, linear animation at some point, be they the quick animations shown between levels in *Pac-Man*, or the high-budget sequences shot on film in *Enter the Matrix*. There is a certain amount of repurposing and remediation going on here, brought on by a nostalgia for previous media and a fear of the pure uniqueness of video gaming. (As McLuhan wrote in the opening pages of *Understanding Media*, the content of any new medium is always another medium.) In these segments, the operator is momentarily irrelevant—in the ambience act the operator was missed; here the operator is forgotten. But instead of being in a perpetual state of no action, the cinematic elements in a game are highly instrumental and deliberate, often carrying the burden of character development or moving the plot along in ways unattainable in normal gameplay. Cinematic interludes transpire within the world of the game and extend the space or narrative of the game in some way. They are outside gameplay, but they are not outside the narrative of gameplay. Formally speaking, cinematic interludes are a type of grotesque fetishization of the game itself as machine. The machine is put at the service of cinema. Scenes are staged and produced from the machine either as rendered video or as procedural, in-game action. Hollywood-style editing and postproduction audio may also be added. So, ironically, what one might consider to be the most purely machinic or "digital" moments in a video game, the discarding of operator and gameplay to create machinima from the raw machine, are at the end of the day the most nongamic. The necessity of the operator-machine relationship becomes all too apparent. These cinematic interludes are a window into the machine itself, oblivious and self-contained.

The actions outlined here are the first step toward a classification system of action in video games. Because they transpire within the imaginary world of the game and are actions instigated by the machine, I will call the first category *diegetic machine acts*. The material aspects of the game environment reside here, as do actions of non-player characters. This moment is the moment of pure process. The machine is up and running—no more, no less.

A Subjective Algorithm

But, of course, video games are not as impersonal and machinic as all this. The operator is as important to the cybernetic phenomenon of video games as the machine itself. So now let us look at an entirely different moment of gamic action. As will become apparent in chapter 4, this second moment is the allegorical stand-in for political intervention, for hacking, and for critique.

The second moment of gamic action refers to a process with spontaneous origins but deliberate ends. This is gamic action as a subjective algorithm. That is to say, in this second moment, video game action is a type of inductive, diachronic patterning of movements executed by individual actors or operators.[12] We are now ready to explore the second quadrant of gamic action: *nondiegetic operator acts*.

These are actions of configuration. They are always executed by the operator and received by the machine. They happen on the exterior of the *world* of the game but are still part of the game software and completely integral to the play of the game. An example: the simplest nondiegetic operator act is pushing Pause. Pausing a game is an action by the operator that sets the entire game into a state of suspended animation. The pause act comes from outside the machine, suspending the game inside a temporary bubble of inactivity. The game freezes in its entirety. It is not simply on hold, as with the ambience act, nor has the machine software crashed. Thus a pause act is undamaging to gameplay and is always reversible, yet the machine itself can never predict when a pause act will happen. It is nondiegetic precisely because nothing in the world of the game can explain or motivate it when it occurs. Pause acts are, in reality, the inverse of what machine actions (as opposed to operator actions) *are*, simply because they negate action, if only temporarily.

Another example of the nondiegetic operator act is the use of cheats or game hacks. Many games have cheats built into them. Often these are deliberately designed into the game for debugging or testing purposes and only later leaked to the public or accidentally discovered by enterprising gamers. Like a pause, the cheat act is executed from outside the world of the game by the operator. It affects the play of the game in some way. This action can be performed with hardware, as with the Game Genie or other physical add-ons, but is more often performed via the software of the actual game, using a special terminal console or simply pressing predetermined button sequences. Shortcuts and tricks can also appear as the result of additional scripts or software, as with the use of macros in *Everquest* or add-ons in *World of Warcraft*, or they can be outright cheats, as in the ability to see through walls in *Counter-Strike*. Cheats are mostly discouraged by the gaming community, for they essentially destroy traditional gameplay by deviating from the established rule set of the game. But macros and add-ons are often tolerated, even encouraged. Likewise the use of a hardware emulator to play a video game can introduce new nondiegetic operator acts (a pause act, for example) even if they did not exist in the original game.

Moving beyond these initial observations on the nondiegetic operator act, one can describe two basic variants. The first is confined to the area of setup. Setup actions exist in all games. They are the interstitial acts of preference setting, game configuration, meta-analysis of gameplay, loading or saving, selecting one player or two, and so on. The pause and cheat acts are both part of this category. It includes all preplay, postplay, and interplay activity.

Yet there exists a second variant of the nondiegetic operator act that is highly important and around which many of the most significant games have been designed. These are gamic actions in which the act of configuration itself *is the very site of gameplay*. These are games oriented around understanding and executing specific algorithms. All resource management simulations, as well as most real-time strategy (RTS) and turn-based games, are designed in this manner. In an RTS game like *Warcraft III*, actions of configuration can take on great importance inside gameplay, not simply before it, as with setup actions. In *Final Fantasy* X the process of configuring various weapons and armor, interacting with the sphere grid, or choosing how the combat will unfold are all executed using interfaces and menus that are not within the diegetic world of the game. These activities may be intimately connected to the narrative of the game, yet they exist in an informatic layer once removed from the pretend play scenario of representational character and story. These actions of configuration are often the very essence of the operator's experience of gameplay—simple proof that gaming may, even for limited moments, eschew the diegetic completely. (As I said in the beginning, the status of the diegetic will be put to the test here; this is one reason why.) Many simulators and turn-based strategy games like *Civilization III* are adept also at using nondiegetic operator acts for large portions of the gameplay.

But why should video games require the operator to become intimate with complex, multipart algorithms and enact them during gameplay? It makes sense to pause for a moment and preview the concept of interpretation that I take up more fully in chapter 4. For this I turn to Clifford Geertz and his gloss on the concept of "deep play." In the essay "Deep Play: Notes on the Balinese Cockfight," Geertz offers a fantastically evocative phrase: "culture, this acted document."[13] There are three interlocked ideas here: There is culture, but culture is a *document*, a text that follows the various logics of a semiotic system, and finally it is an *acted* document. This places culture on quite a different footing than other nonacted semiotic systems. (Certainly with literature or cinema there are important connections to the action of the author, or with the structure of discourse and its acted utterances, or with the action of reading, but *as texts* they are not action-based media in the same sense that culture is and, I suggest here, video games are. Geertz's observation, then, is not to say that culture is a text but to say that *action is a text*. In subsequent years this has resonated greatly in cultural studies, particularly in theories of performance.) In "Deep Play," Geertz describes play as a cultural

Final Fantasy X, Squaresoft, 2001

phenomenon that has meaning. Because play is a cultural act and because action is textual, play is subject to interpretation just like any other text. The concept of "depth" refers to the way in which the more equally matched a cockfight becomes, the more unpredictable and volatile the outcome might be. The closer one is to an adversary, the more likely that entire reputations will be built or destroyed upon the outcome of the fight. So, in identifying deep play, Geertz demonstrates how something entirely outside play can be incorporated into it and expressed through it:

> What makes Balinese cockfighting deep is thus not money in itself, but what, the more of it that is involved the more so, money causes to happen: the migration of the Balinese status hierarchy into the body of the cockfight. . . . The cocks may be surrogates for their owners' personalities, animal mirrors of psychic form, but the cockfight is— or more exactly, deliberately is made to be—a simulation of the social matrix, the involved system of cross-cutting, overlapping, highly corporate groups—villages, kingroups, irrigation societies, temple congregations, "castes"—in which its devotees live. And as prestige, the necessity to affirm it, defend it, celebrate it, justify it, and just plain bask in it (but not, given the strongly ascriptive character of Balinese stratification, to seek it), is perhaps the central driving force in the society, so also—ambulant penises, blood sacrifices, and monetary exchanges aside—is it of the cockfight. This apparent amusement and seeming sport is, to take another phrase from Erving Goffman, "a status bloodbath."[14]

Play is a symbolic action for larger issues in culture. It is the expression of structure. "The cockfight is a means of expression," he writes.[15] It is an aesthetic, enacted vehicle for "a powerful rendering of life."[16]

I want to suggest that a very similar thing is happening in *Final Fantasy* X or *The Sims*. Acts of configuration in video games express processes in culture that are large, unknown, dangerous, and painful, but they do not express them directly. "The playful nip denotes the bite," wrote Gregory Bateson, "but it does not denote what would be denoted by the bite."[17] Acts of configuration are a rendering of life: the transformation into an information economy in the United States since the birth of video games as a mass medium in the 1970s has precipitated massive upheavals in the lives of individuals submitted to a process of retraining and redeployment into a new economy mediated by machines and other informatic artifacts. This transformation has been the subject of much reflection, in the work of everyone from Fredric Jameson to Manuel Castells. The new "general equivalent" of information has changed the way culture is created and experienced. The same quantitative modulations and numerical valuations required by the new information worker are thus observed in a dazzling array of new cultural phenomena, from the cut-up sampling culture of hip-hop to the calculus curves of computer-aided architectural design. In short, to live today is to know how to use menus. Acts of configuration in video games are but a footnote to this general transformation. So the second classification of gamic actions I have proposed, nondiegetic operator acts, follows the same logic revealed in Geertz's analysis of the Balinese cockfight, or indeed Marx's understanding of social labor: just as the commodity form carries within it a map for understanding all the larger contradictions of life under capitalism, and just as the cockfight is a site for enacting various dramas of social relations, so these nondiegetic operator acts in video games are an allegory for the algorithmic structure of today's informatic culture. Video games render social realities into playable form. I will return to this theme in chapter 4.

With these first two moments of gamic action in mind, one can begin to see the first steps toward a classification system. The first moment of gamic action revealed diegetic machine acts, while the second moment revealed nondiegetic operator acts. I can now put together the first two axes in the classification scheme, pairing diegetic opposite nondiegetic and machine opposite operator.

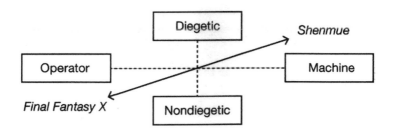

The first two moments of gamic action therefore explore one of the diagonal relationships in this diagram. (Some of the other relationships in the diagram will be examined shortly.) The first diagonal relationship is between (1) the action experience of being at the mercy of abstract informatic rules (the atmosphere of the ambience act in *Shenmue*) and (2) the action experience of structuring subjective play, of working with rules and configurations (configuring and executing plans in *Final Fantasy X*). One motion emanates outward from the machine, while the other proceeds inward into the machine. One deals with the process of informatics, and the other deals with the informatics of process. Like *Shenmue*, the artfulness of games like *Myst* or *Ico* is their ability to arrest the desires of the operator in a sort of poetry of the algorithm. The experience of ambience, of nonplay, is always beckoning in *Ico*. Yet in nonplay, the operator is in fact moving his or her experience closer to the actual rhythms of the machine. In this way, the desires of the operator are put into a state of submission at the hands of the desires of the machine. This same masochistic fascination is evident in *Myst*. One doesn't play *Myst* so much as one submits to it. Its intricate puzzles and lush renderings achieve

Ico, Sony Computer Entertainment, 2001

equivalent results in this sense. But with *Warcraft III* or *Civilization III* or any number of simulation games and RTSs, the contrapositive action experience occurs: instead of penetrating into the logic of the machine, the operator hovers above the game, one step removed from its diegesis, tweaking knobs and adjusting menus. Instead of being submissive, one speaks of these as "God games." Instead of experiencing the algorithm as algorithm, one *enacts* the algorithm. In both cases, the operator has a distinct relationship to informatics, but it is a question of the composition of that relationship. *Shenmue* is an experience of informatics from within, whereas *Final Fantasy X* is an experience of informatics from above. Of course, the axes of my diagram still hold: *Shenmue* is primarily a game played by a machine, while *Final Fantasy X* is primarily a game played by an operator; and likewise *Shenmue* situates gameplay primarily in diegetic space, while *Final Fantasy X* situates gameplay primarily in nondiegetic space.

The Dromenon

I have waited thus far to engage directly with the twin concepts of "play" and "game," perhaps at my peril, in order to convey the bounded utility of the two terms. As stated at the outset, a game is an activity defined by rules in which players try to reach some sort of goal. As for play, the concept is one of the least theorized, despite being so central to human activity.[18] Huizinga's work in the 1930s, culminating in his book *Homo Ludens,* and Caillois's 1958 book *Man, Play, and Games* both analyze play as a social and cultural phenomenon.

> Play is a voluntary activity or occupation executed within certain fixed limits of time and place, according to rules freely accepted but absolutely binding, having its aim in itself and accompanied by a feeling of tension, joy and the consciousness that it is "different" from "ordinary life."[19]

This definition, from Huizinga, is the distillation of his observations on the nature of play: that it is free, that it is not part of ordinary life, that it is secluded in time and place, that it creates order (in the form of rules), and that it promotes the formation of communities of players. Caillois, revealing an unlikely intellectual debt to the earlier book (Caillois was a leftist and friends with the likes of Georges

Bataille; Huizinga was a cultural historian in the old school), agrees almost point for point with Huizinga on the definition of play: "It appears to be an activity that is (1) free, (2) separate, (3) uncertain, (4) unproductive, (5) regulated, and (6) fictive."[20]

Huizinga makes overtures for play being a part of human life in its many details. He argues for a direct connection to be made between play and culture, that play is not simply something that exists within culture, but on the contrary that culture arises in and through play. "We have to conclude," he writes, "that civilization is, in its earliest phases, played. It does not come *from* play like a babe detaching itself from the womb: it arises *in* and *as* play, and never leaves it"; or earlier in the text, "Culture arises in the form of play. . . . It is played from the very beginning."[21] But at the same time, Huizinga pays little attention to the material details of this or that individual moment of play. Instead he takes the concept of play as primary, stripping from it anything inessential. His rationale is that one must never start from the assumption that play is defined through something that is *not* play,[22] and hence play for Huizinga becomes unassigned and detached, articulated in its essential form but rarely in actual form as game or medium. In the end, it is the very irreducibility of play for Huizinga—the natural purity of it—that makes play less useful for an analysis of the specificity of video games as a medium. His book is so far removed from the medium that it can merely gesture a way forward, not provide a core approach.

While Huizinga and Caillois generally agree on the question of play, what distinguishes them is this: Caillois moves beyond the formal definition of play, which he claims is "opposed to reality," and moves further to describe the "unique, irreducible characteristics" of games in their "multitude and infinite variety."[23] This more materialist approach is where Caillois is most at home. He proceeds to map out four basic types of games (competitive, chance, mimicry, and panic or "vertigo" games), each of which may fluctuate along a continuum from whimsical improvisation to being rule bound. And unlike Huizinga, Caillois is not hesitant to mention actual games, as well as play activities, and group them together according to various traits. So in Caillois we have an attention to football and roulette, to kite flying and traveling carnivals.

But what Huizinga and Caillois have in common, and what confines their usefulness to the present single moment of gamic action, is that they both focus specifically on the individual's experience during play. As sociologists, they naturally privilege the human realm over the technological realm; play is an "occupation" or "activity" of humans (and also of some animals). As theorists of play, they naturally regard nonplay as beside the question. This is fine for understanding "play" or "game" in general, but it only partially suffices for understanding video games as a specific historical medium with definite tangible qualities. I have already described how in the ambience act, gameplay is essentially suspended, but does this mean that the ambience act is not part of what it means to play a video game? Or I have also described the use of hacks and cheats as nondiegetic operator acts, which both Huizinga and Caillois would argue by definition threaten play (cheaters are "spoil-sports," claims Huizinga), but does this mean that hacks and cheats are not part of what it means to play a video game? If the object of one's analysis is a medium in its entirety, must only those aspects of the medium that resemble play or a game be considered? Such an approach elevates an understanding of "play" or "game" pure and simple but, in doing so, ignores the vast detail of the medium in general. To arrive at a definition of video games, then, one must take Huizinga and Caillois's concept of play and view it as it is actually embedded inside algorithmic game machines.[24] This different approach, owing more to media studies than to cultural anthropology, tries to work backward from the material at hand, approaching the medium in its entirety rather than as an instantiation of a specific element of human activity. Only then may one start to sift through the various traces and artifacts of video gaming in order to arrive at a suitable framework for interpreting it. This is why I do not begin this book with Huizinga and Caillois, as any number of approaches would, but instead situate them here in this third moment, in the intersection of the playing agent and the diegetic space of gameplay.

This third moment illuminates action in the way that action is most conventionally defined, as the deliberate movements of an individual. Here Huizinga's understanding of the play element in sacred performances is revealing:

The rite is a *dromenon*, which means "something acted," an act, action. That which is enacted, or the stuff of action, is a *drama*, which again means act, action represented on a stage. Such action may occur as a performance or a contest. The rite, or "ritual act" represents a cosmic happening, an event in the natural process. The word "represents," however, does not cover the exact meaning of the act, at least not in its looser, modern connotation; for here "representation" is really *identification*, the mystic repetition or *re-presentation* of the event. The rite produces the effect which is then not so much *shown figuratively* as *actually reproduced* in the action. The function of the rite, therefore, is far from being merely imitative; it causes the worshippers to participate in the sacred happening itself.[25]

Representation is a question of figuratively reshowing an action, Huizinga suggests, while play is an effect reproduced *in* the action. The dromenon, the ritual act, is thus helpful for understanding the third moment of gamic action: the *diegetic operator act*. This is the moment of direct operator action inside the imaginary world of gameplay, and it is the part of my schema that overlaps most with Huizinga and Caillois.

Diegetic operator acts are diegetic because they take place within the world of gameplay; they are operator acts because they are perpetrated by the game player rather than the game software or any outside force. Diegetic operator acts appear as either *move acts* or *expressive acts* (two categories that are more variations on a theme than mutually exclusive). Simply put, move acts change the physical position or orientation of the game environment. This may mean a translation of the player character's position in the game world, or it may mean the movement of the player character's gaze such that new areas of the game world are made visible. Move acts are commonly effected by using a joystick or analog stick, or any type of movement controller. In many video games, move acts appear in the form of player character motion: running, jumping, driving, strafing, crouching, and so on; but also in games like *Tetris* where the player does not have a strict player character avatar, move acts still come in the form of spatial translation, rotation, stacking, and interfacing of game tokens.

But parallel to this in operator gameplay is a kind of gamic act that, simply, concerns player *expression*. Even a single mouse click counts

Tony Hawk's Pro Skater 4, Neversoft, 2002

here. These are actions such as select, pick, get, rotate, unlock, open, talk, examine, use, fire, attack, cast, apply, type, emote. Expressive acts can be rather one-dimensional in certain game genres (the expressive act of firing in *Quake* or *Unreal*, for example), or highly complex, as in the case of object selection and combination in strategy or adventure games.

Some games merge these various expressive acts. In *Metroid Prime*, firing one's weapon is used interchangeably both to attack and to open doors. In fact, experientially these acts are equivalent: they both exert an expressive desire outward from the player character to objects in the world that are deemed actionable. That one expressive act opens a door and another kills a nonplayer character is insignificant from the perspective of gamic action. What is important is the coupling of acting agent (the player character) and actionable object.

Not everything in a game is available to the expressive act. There are actionable objects and nonactionable objects. Additionally, objects can change their actionable status. For example, an Alien Slave in *Half-Life* is actionable when alive but nonactionable when killed, or a gold mine in *Warcraft III* is actionable when producing but not when collapsed. Actionable objects may come in the form of buttons, blocks, keys, obstacles, doors, words, nonplayer characters, and so on. So in a text-based game like *Adventure*, actionable objects come in the form of specific object names that must be examined or used, whereas in *Metroid Prime* actionable objects are often revealed to the operator via the scan visor, or in *Deus Ex* actionable objects are highlighted by the HUD. Nonactionable objects are inert scenery. No amount of effort will garner results from nonactionable objects. The actionability of objects is determined when the game's levels are designed. Certain objects are created as inert masses, while others are connected to specific functions in the game that produce action responses. (During level design, some machine acts are also specified, such as spawn points, lights, shaders, and hazards.) Available expressive-act objects tend to have different levels of significance for different genres of games. Adventure games like *The Longest Journey* require keen attention to the action status of objects in the visual field. But in RTS games or first-person shooters, discovering the actionability of new objects is not a primary goal of gameplay; instead these genres hinge on interaction with known action objects, typically some combination of ammo, health packs, and monsters.

This discussion of diegetic operator acts, and the one before it on nondiegetic, may be documented through a sort of archaeological exploration of game controller design. Game controllers instantiate these two types of acts as buttons, sticks, triggers, and other input devices. So while there is an imaginative form of the expressive act within the diegesis of the game, there is also a physical form of the same act. In a PC-based game like *Half-Life*, the operator acts are literally inscribed on various regions of the keyboard and mouse. The mouse ball movement is devoted to move acts, but the mouse buttons are for expressive acts. Likewise, certain clusters of keyboard keys (A, W, S, D, Space, and Ctrl) are for move acts, while others (R, E, F) are for expressive acts. But this physical inscription is also variable. While certain controller buttons, such as the PlayStation's Start and Select buttons, are used almost exclusively for nondiegetic operator acts, controller buttons often do double duty, serving in one capacity during certain gamic logics and in another capacity during others. For example, the Atari 2600 joystick, a relatively simple controller with button and directional stick, must facilitate all in-game operator acts.

The Play of the Structure

In "Structure, Sign and Play in the Discourse of the Human Sciences," Jacques Derrida focuses on the concept of play. He writes about how things "come into play," and refers to "the *play* of the structure," or the "play of signification," or even simply "the play of the world."[26] Or in *Dissemination*, he writes of the "play of a syntax," or the "play" of "a chain of significations."[27] So at a basic level, play is simply how things transpire linguistically for Derrida, how, in a general sense, they happen to happen. But the concept is more sophisticated than it might seem, for it gets at the very nature of language. After citing Claude Lévi-Strauss on the practical impossibility of arriving at a total understanding of language, that one can never accurately duplicate the speech of a people without exhaustively recounting every word said in the past, words in circulation today, as well as all words to come, Derrida seizes on this type of useless pursuit of totality to further explain his sense of the word "play":

> Totalization, therefore, is sometimes defined as *useless*, and sometimes as *impossible*. This is no doubt due to the fact that there are two ways of conceiving the limit of totalization. And I assert once more that these two determinations coexist in a non-expressed way in Lévi-Strauss's discourse. Totalization can be judged impossible in the classical style: one then refers to the empirical endeavor of either a subject or a finite discourse hopelessly panting after an infinite richness that it can never master. There is too much and more than one can say.

Then Derrida shifts to play.

> But nontotalization can also be determined in another way: no longer from the standpoint of a concept of finitude as relegation to the empirical, but from the standpoint of the concept of *play* [*jeu*]. If totalization no longer has any meaning, it is not because the infiniteness of a field cannot be covered by a finite glance or a finite discourse, but because the nature of the field—that is, language and a finite language—excludes totalization: this field is in effect that of a *game* [*jeu*], that is to say, of a field of infinite substitutions in the closing of a finite group. This field only allows these infinite substitutions because it is finite, that is to say, because instead of being an incommensurable field, as in the classical hypothesis, instead of being too large, there is something missing from it: a center which arrests and grounds the play of substitutions. One could say—rigorously using that word whose scandalous signification is always obliterated in French—that this movement of play, permitted by the lack, the absence of center or origin, is the movement of *supplementarity*.[28]

The field of language is therefore not quantitatively but *qualitatively* inadequate. It is a question not of enlarging the field but of refashioning it internally. This process of remaking is what Derrida calls the movement of play.[29] Using the logic of supplementarity, play reconstitutes the field, not to create a new wholeness but to enforce a sort of permanent state of nonwholeness, or "nontotalization." Play is a sort of permanent agitation of the field, a generative motion filling in the structure itself, compensating for it, but also supplementing and sustaining it. "Transformative play," write Katie Salen and Eric Zimmerman, "is a special case of play that occurs when the free movement of play alters the more rigid structure in which it takes place."[30] Derrida describes this generative agitation as follows:

> Play is the disruption of presence. . . . Turned towards the lost or impossible presence of the absent origin, [Lévi-Strauss's] structuralist thematic of broken immediacy is therefore the saddened, *negative*, nostalgic, guilty, Rousseauistic side of the thinking of play whose other side would be the Nietzschean *affirmation*, the joyous affirmation of the world in play and of the innocence in becoming, the affirmation of a world of signs without fault, without truth, and without origin which is offered to an active interpretation. *This affirmation then determines the* non-center *otherwise than as loss of the center.* And it plays without security. For there is a *sure* play: that which is limited to the *substitution of given and existing, present,* pieces. In absolute chance, affirmation also surrenders itself to *genetic* indetermination, to the *seminal* adventure of the trace.[31]

So although it is one of his most prized pieces of terminology, Derrida doesn't as much say what play is as use the concept of play to explain the nature of something else, namely, the structure of language. The word is lucky enough to be placed alongside other of Derrida's privileged concepts; it is paired in this section with the supplement and the trace. And in *Dissemination,* the concept of play is described in such broad strokes and in such close proximity to writing itself that one might easily swap one term for the other. After describing the relationship between playfulness and seriousness in Plato, Derrida observes, "As soon as it comes into being and into language, play *erases itself as such.* Just as writing must erase itself as such before truth, etc. The point is that there *is* no *as such* where writing or play are concerned."[32] Play is, in this way, crucial to both language and signification, even if play erases itself in the act of bringing the latter concepts into existence.

So it comes full circle. With Huizinga, play was held aloft as a thoroughly axiomatic concept, irreducible to anything more phenomenologically primitive. But with Geertz, the pure concept is put to the rigors of a close reading, as any other textual form might be. And now with Derrida one is back to the concept of play as pure positivity. If

Geertz's goal is the interpretation of play, then Derrida's goal is the play of interpretation. Play brings out for Derrida a certain sense of generative agitation or ambiguity, a way of joyfully moving forward without being restricted by the retrograde structures of loss or absence. And like Maurice Blondel's coupling of truth with action, Derrida sought to replace so-called textual truth with the generative tensions of active reading.

Now we are prepared to consider the fourth type of gamic action, that of *nondiegetic machine acts*. These are actions performed by the machine and integral to the entire experience of the game but not contained within a narrow conception of the world of gameplay. This is the most interesting category. Included here are internal forces like power-ups, goals, high-score stats, dynamic difficulty adjustment (DDA), the HUD, and health packs, but also external forces exerted (knowingly or unknowingly) by the machine such as software crashes, low polygon counts, temporary freezes, server downtime, and network lag. I say "narrow conception" because many nondiegetic machine acts such as power-ups or health packs are in fact incorporated directly into the narrative of necessities in the game such that the line between what is diegetic and what is nondiegetic becomes quite indistinct.

The most emblematic nondiegetic machine act is "game over," the moment of gamic death. While somewhat determined by the performance of the operator, or lack thereof, death acts are levied fundamentally by the game itself, in response to the input and over the contestation of the operator. A death act is the moment when the controller stops accepting the user's gameplay and essentially turns off (at least temporarily until the game can segue to a menu act or straight back to gameplay). This moment usually coincides with the death of the operator's player character inside the game environment (or otherwise with the violation of specific rules, as when missions are called off in *Splinter Cell*). The games created by Jodi are perfect experiments in nondiegetic machine acts in general and death acts in particular. The code of the machine itself is celebrated, with all its illegibility, disruptiveness, irrationality, and impersonalness. Jodi are what Huizinga calls spoilsports, meaning that their games intentionally deviate from the enchanting order created by the game:

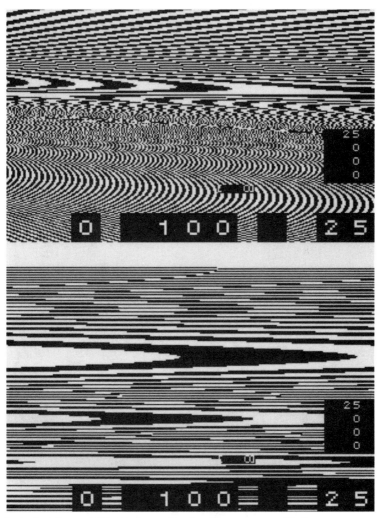

Jodi, *Ctrl-Space*, 1998–99. Reproduced with permission of Jodi.

Inside the play-ground an absolute and peculiar order reigns. Here we come across another, very positive feature of play: it creates order, *is* order. Into an imperfect world and into the confusion of life it brings a temporary, a limited perfection. Play demands order absolute and supreme. The least deviation from it "spoils the game," robs it of its character and makes it worthless.... Play casts a spell over us; it is "enchanting," "captivating."[33]

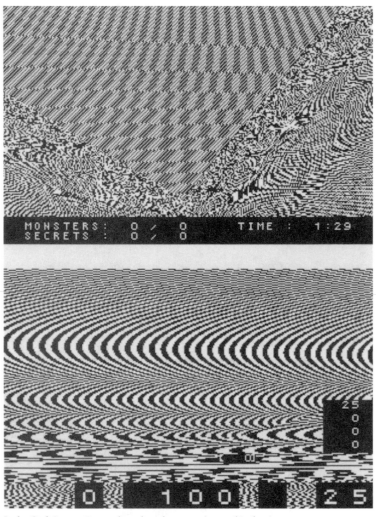

Jodi, *Ctrl-Space*. Reproduced with permission of Jodi.

I cite this passage to highlight the dramatic disagreement between Huizinga's position and that of Derrida (or Jodi, if one was foolish enough to request they take a position on things). With Huizinga is the notion that play must in some sense create order, but with Derrida is the notion that play is precisely the deviation from order, or further the perpetual inability to achieve order, and hence never wanting it in the first place. Admittedly, the "game over" of a game is not *affirmative*, to use Derrida's Nietzschean terminology, but it is certainly noncentering, putting the gamer into a temporary state of disability and submission.

The death act is, properly placed, part of the first type of nondiegetic machine acts that I will call the *disabling act*. These actions are any type of gamic aggression or gamic deficiency that arrives from outside the world of the game and infringes negatively on the game in some way. They can be fatal or temporary, necessary or unnecessary. So, as mentioned, all the following phenomena are included: crashes, low polygon counts, bugs, slowdowns, temporary freezes, and network lag. No action is more irritating to the gamer. Following Huizinga, these actions have the ability to destroy the game from without, to disable its logic. But at the same time, they are often the most constitutive category of game acts, for they have the ability to define the outer boundaries of aesthetics in gaming, the degree zero for an entire medium.

The second type of nondiegetic machine act comprises any number of actions offered by the machine that enrich the operator's gameplay rather than degrade it. These should be called *enabling acts*. They are the absolute essence of smooth runtime in gameplay. With an enabling act, the game machine grants something to the operator: a piece of information, an increase in speed, temporary invulnerability, an extra life, increased health, a teleportation portal, points, cash, or some other bonus. Thus receipt or use of the aforementioned items—power-ups, goals, the HUD (excluding any input elements), and health packs—all constitute enabling acts. The functionality of objects, or their *actionality*, must be taken into account when considering the status of enabling acts. Inert objects are not included here. This category is the most clear contrapositive to the diegetic operator acts discussed earlier.

It is perhaps important to stress that, while many of these enabling acts are the center of most games, they exist in an uneasy relationship to the diegetic world of the game. In fact, many enabling objects in games are integrated seamlessly into the world of the game using some sort of trick or disguise—what Eddo Stern calls "metaphorically patched artifacts"[34]—as with the voice recorders that are used as save stations in *The Thing* or the HEV suit charging stations that supplement health in *Half-Life* (or even erased from the object world of the game, as with the act of leaning against a wall to regain health in *The Getaway*). Thus the "xyzzy" command in *Adventure*, which teleports the player character to and from home base, is technically a nondiegetic machine act, but its nondiegetic status is covered over by the narrative of the game, which insists that the command is a magic spell, and thus, although it is nondiegetic, the command cooperates with the diegesis rather than threatening it. The same xyzzy logic is at work with the taxis in *Vice City* that, after the player character dies, transport him back to the previous mission. This wormhole through space and time reveals the tension often present in games whereby diegetic objects are used as a mask to obfuscate nondiegetic (but necessary) play functions.

Beyond the disabling and enabling acts, there is an additional category of nondiegetic machine acts worth mentioning. These are any number of *machinic embodiments* that emanate outward from a game to exert their own logic on the gamic form. For example, the graphic design of the aliens in the Atari 2600 version of *Space Invaders* is a direct embodiment of how a byte of data, equivalent to eight zero-or-one bits, may be represented as a strip of eight pixels turned on or off. The alien invaders are nothing more than a series of byte strips stacked together.[35] This is math made visible.

The shape and size of Mario in the NES version of *Super Mario Bros.* is determined not simply by artistic intention or narrative logic but by the design specifications of the 8-bit 6502 microchip driving the game software. Only a certain number of colors can be written to the NES screen at one time, and thus the design of Mario follows the logic of the machine by using only specific colors and specific palettes. But this is not a simple determinism on the macro scale of what exists on the micro scale. There are also other influences from the logic of informatics that affect the nature of certain gamic actions. One example is multithreading and object-oriented programming that creates the conditions of possibility for certain formal outcomes in the game. When one plays *State of Emergency*, the swarm effect of

Space Invaders alien as stack of ten bytes

rioting is a formal action enacted by the game on the experience of gameplay and incorporated into the game's narrative. Yet the formal quality of swarming as such is still nondiegetic to the extent that it finds its genesis primarily in the current logic of informatics (emergence, social networks, artificial life, and so on) rather than in any necessary element in the narrative, itself enlisted to "explain" and incorporate this nondiegetic force into the story line (a riot) after the fact.

Other transformations in material culture may also reappear in games as nondiegetic emanations. Consider the difference between arcade games and home computer or console games. Arcade games are generally installed in public spaces and require payment to play. Computer and console games, on the other hand, exist primarily in the home and are typically free to play once purchased. This material difference has tended to structure the narrative flow of games in two very different ways. Arcade games are often designed around the concept of lives, while console games are designed around health. For example, in arcade *Pac-Man,* a single quarter gives the player a fixed number of lives, whereas in *SOCOM* the player must maintain health above zero or else die. Arcade games are characterized by a more quantized set of penalties and limitations on play: one quarter equals a certain number of lives. Console and computer games, by contrast, offer a more fluid continuum of gameplay based on replenishment and on of a qualitative resource. Save stations extend this logic onsole and computer platforms, resulting in a more continuous, unrepeating sense of gameplay. And at the same moment in history, one may document the invention of the pause act as a standard feature of video games (the pause act is essentially absent from the arcade). *Super Mario Bros.*, which was released first for the arcade and then, famously, for the home console Nintendo Entertainment System, exists on the threshold between these two nondiegetic machine embodiments. On the one hand, the game retains the concept of lives familiar to the arcade format, but on the other hand, the game uses a variety of power-ups that strengthen the relative vitality of any single life. A single Mario life may be augmented and crippled several times before being killed outright, thereby exhibiting a primitive version of what would later be known as health. *Super Mario Bros.* was not the first game to do this, but it remains emblematic of this transformation in the early to mid-1980s. Games like *Gauntlet* accomplished the reverse: the game remained popular as an arcade game, yet it used an innovative technique whereby quarters bought health rather than lives.

It is in this sense that Derrida's conception of play becomes quite important, for nondiegetic machine acts can be defined as those elements that create a generative *agitation* or ambiguity—what Genette calls metalepsis—between the inside of the game and the outside of the game, between what constitutes the essential core of the game and what causes that illusion (literally, "in-play") to be undone. The lives-health distinction (or the graphic design of 8-bit sprites) did not impinge on the various narratives of arcade and early home games— they are well motivated in gameplay, but in many cases nondiegetic machine acts are consummate unplay, particularly when dealing with crashes and lags celebrated in the Jodi variant. Still, this does not exempt them from being absolutely intertwined with the notion of play. *Metal Gear Solid* celebrates this inside-outside agitation with the boss Psycho Mantis. The villain's supposed powers of mind control are so powerful that they break out of the game console entirely, at times pretending to interrupt the normal functioning of the television display. Mantis also uses his psychic powers to refer to other games that the player has played, a trick enabled by surreptitiously

scanning files on the console's memory card. Then, in the most griev-
ous violation of diegetic illusion, the player is required physically to
move the game controller from port one to port two on the console
in order to defeat Mantis. This brief moment of unplay does not
destroy the game but in fact elevates it to a higher form of play. Even
if the player does not believe that Mantis is a true psychic, the use
of nondiegetic machine acts—requiring, in response, a nondiegetic
operator act to continue playing—remains effective precisely because
it follows the loop of supplementarity described in Derrida. The narrative follows faithfully enough to explain breaking the diegesis, and
after the short diversion the player is safely returned to normal gameplay. Several other narrative games such as *Max Payne* contain similar "Mantis moments" where the game deliberately breaks the fourth
wall. In a strange, drug-induced state, the Payne character breaks out
of the diegetic space of the game to view himself as a sort of mari-
onette within the world of gameplay:

MAX'S WIFE (voice-over): You are in a computer game, Max.

MAX (voice-over): The truth was a burning green crack through
my brain. Weapon statistics hanging in the air, glimpsed out of the
corner of my eye. Endless repetition of the act of shooting, time
slowing down to show off my moves. The paranoid feel of someone
controlling my every step. *I was in a computer game.* Funny as hell, it
was the most horrible thing I could think of.[36]

This generative agitation may be explored further by looking at
the interface of the first-person shooter. There are two layers at play
here that would seem to contradict and disable each other. The first
is the full volume of the world, extending in three dimensions, varied, spatial, and textured. The second is the HUD, which exists in a
flat plane and is overlayed on top of the first world. This second layer
benefits from none of the richness, dynamic motion, or narrative illusion of the first layer (a few notable counterexamples like *Metroid
Prime* notwithstanding). The HUD has instead a sort of static, informatic permanence, offering information or giving various updates to
the operator. In Derrida's vocabulary, the HUD exists as a supplement
to the rendered world. It completes it, but only through a process of
exteriority that is unable again to penetrate its core. The HUD is
uncomfortable in its two-dimensionality, but forever there it will stay, in

a relationship of incommensurability with the world of the game, and a metaphor for the very nature of play itself. The play of the nondiegetic machine act is therefore a play within the various semiotic layers of the video game. It is form playing with other form.

One should always speak of waning agitations or waxing agitations. In the diegetic machine act, the intensities of gameplay slow to near equilibrium, but at that same moment the game world is full of action and energy. The diegetic operator act is also defined through intensities, or *vectors* of agitation: the time-based unfolding of a game is never smooth or consistent but is instead marked by a wide variance in the agitation of movement, whereby one moment may be quite placid and unagitated, but another moment may be saturated with motion and violence. Often these differences in intensities are incorporated directly into gameplay—the shadows versus the light in *Manhunt*, for example, or the intensities of safe spaces versus hostile spaces in *Halo*. Nondiegetic operator acts, defined as they were in terms of configuration, are also about probabilistic customization and local calibrations of options and numbers (the depletion and augmentation of statistical parameters like hunger and energy in *The Sims*). And, as discussed, nondiegetic machine acts are about the various intensities of agitation between the various layers of the game itself, whether it be the agitation between two- and three-dimensionality, or between connectivity and disconnectivity, or between gameplay and the lack thereof. Games are always about getting from here to there. They require local differentials of space and action, not an abstract navigation through a set of anchored points of reference.

Taking all four moments together, one may revisit the earlier diagram. This is an incomplete diagram in many ways. To be thorough, one should supplement it with a consideration of the relationship between two or more operators in a multiplayer game, for the very concept of diegetic space becomes quite complicated with the addition of multiple players. Likewise the machine should most likely be rendered internally complex so that the game world could be considered in distinction to the game engine driving it. Nevertheless, the active experience of gaming is here displayed via four different moments of gamic action.

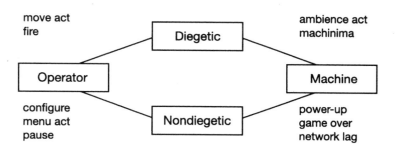

The interpretive framework presented in this chapter aims to be as inclusive as possible. I have deliberately avoided the assumption—incorrect, in my view—that video games are merely games that people play on computers. Such a position leads to a rather one-dimensional view of what video games are. I have also tried to avoid privileging either play or narrative, another tendency that is common in other approaches. There are many significant aspects of gaming that happen completely outside play proper (e.g., the setup act) or are not part of a traditional narrative (e.g., machinic embodiments). Thus I suggest that video games are complex, active media that may involve both humans and computers and may transpire both inside diegetic space and outside diegetic space.

In sum, because of my starting assumption—that video games are not just images or stories or play or games but *actions*—I have outlined a four-part system for understanding action in video games: gaming is a pure process made knowable in the machinic resonance of diegetic machine acts; gaming is a subjective algorithm, a code intervention exerted from both within gameplay and without gameplay in the form of the nondiegetic operator act; gaming is a ritualistic dromenon of players transported to the imaginary place of gameplay, and acted out in the form of diegetic operator acts; and gaming is the play of the structure, a generative agitation between inside and outside effected through the nondiegetic machine act. A theoretical analogue for the first moment would be the vitality of pure matter, the machinic phylum. For the second, it would be political intervention, hacking, critique, outside thought. The third would be desire, utopia, and the social. And a theoretical analogue for the fourth moment would be

Gamic Action

Type of gamic action	Categories	Shape of action	Quality of action	Emblematic games
Diegetic machine act	Ambience act, machinima	Process	Informatic, atmospheric	*Ico, Myst, Shenmue*
Nondiegetic operator act	Acts of configuration, setup act	Algorithm	Simulation, material	*Warcraft III, Flight Simulator, Final Fantasy X*
Diegetic operator act	Movement act, expressive act	Play	Rule-based, singular	*Tekken, Metroid Prime, Half-Life*
Nondiegetic machine act	Disabling act, enabling act, machinic embodiments	Code	Swarms, patterning, relationality	*Dance Dance Revolution, SOD, State of Emergency*

écriture, the supplement, the new. These are four moments, four suggestions. They should in no way be thought of as fixed "rules" for video games, but instead are tendencies seen to arise through the examination of the particular games listed here at this time. These are not ideal types; they are, rather, provisional observations that spring from an analysis of the material specificities of the medium.

2

Origins of the First-Person Shooter

The beginning of a medium is that historical moment when something ceases to represent itself. "The theater brings onto the rectan-
gle of the stage, one after the other, a whole series of places that are
foreign to one another," wrote Foucault in one of his infrequent for-
ays into aesthetics. "Thus it is that the cinema is a very odd rectangular room, at the end of which, on a two-dimensional screen, one
sees the projection of a three-dimensional space."[1] The movie theater
is a complex intersection of seemingly incommensurate media environments: a three-dimensional space is used for viewing a two-
dimensional plane that in turn represents the illusion of another three-
dimensional space. Likewise today the cinema is butting up against
another seemingly incommensurate medium, the video game. They
are no less different as two dimensions are from three. Yet it is a cliché
today to claim that movies are becoming more and more like video
games. What exactly does such a claim mean? Today video games
and film are influencing and incorporating each other in novel ways.
Through a historical transformation that he calls the "automation of
sight," Lev Manovich writes how the camera has adopted a more and

more machinic gaze with the passage into the digital.[2] One witnesses this transformation firsthand in the clinical, disembodied tracking shots in *Panic Room*, or in the digital effects of *The Matrix*, itself often criticized for looking too much like a video game.

But ignoring for a moment all the pizzazz of digital effects in moviemaking, there exists a much simpler visual technique that one may use to examine how cinema and gaming are constituted as similar and dissimilar media formats: the use of the first-person subjective camera angle. I would like to explore this shift through the following proposition: In film, the subjective perspective is marginalized and used primarily to effect a sense of alienation, detachment, fear, or violence, while in games the subjective perspective is quite common and used to achieve an intuitive sense of motion and action in gameplay. This claim will most certainly rankle some readers, so I should first clarify a few things before continuing.

The Subjective Shot

Generally speaking, film technique involves the staging of action by characters and the recording of that action by elements of the film apparatus. Paul Willemen, in his essay "The Fourth Look," has described the various visual axes that exist in a typical filmic scenario: the camera's look, the audience's look, the intradiegetic look between characters, and the fourth look, "the look at the viewer" by an onscreen character.[3] In the classical Hollywood style, the first and second looks are often subordinated to the third. The fourth look is generally avoided, since it forces the viewer to confront his or her own voyeuristic position.[4] However, occasionally the strict separation of these four looks is not so carefully observed. Occasionally, two of the looks—the look of the camera and the look of a single character—merge together, so that the camera lens and the eyes of a character become one. This results in a rather extreme first-person point-of-view shot, where the camera pans and tracks as if it were mounted on the neck of a character. When the camera fuses with a character's body, the viewer sees *exactly* what the character sees, as if the camera "eye" were the same as the character "I." The camera merges with the character both visually and subjectively. In a sense, this type of first-person shot is the spatial opposite of Willemen's fourth look. They are like two vectors, one pointing outward and one pointing inward. They constitute a grand axis that extends outward from the viewer's eyes, pierces the screen, enters the diegesis of the film, and backs out again. It is this grand axis that creates so much difficulty in cinema. The difficulty is so great that both types of shot are largely avoided, and when they are used, they signify a problematic form of vision (which I will describe later).

It is important to stress the difference between the subjective shot (when the camera shows what the actual eyes of a character would see) and the more general point-of-view (POV) shot. POV shots show approximately what a character would see. They show the perspective more or less from the character's vantage point. Yet subjective shots mean to show the exact physiological or emotional qualities of what a character would see. In other words, the POV shot tends to hover abstractly in space at roughly the same diegetic location of a character. But the subjective shot very precisely positions itself inside the skull of that character. It is a question less of type than of degree.

The POV shot is most commonly illustrated by considering the shot/reverse-shot sequence in which a character is first shown looking at something, and then the camera swings in reverse to a POV shot to see what he or she was looking at. Correct eyeline matching is employed to create the illusion of a coherent visual space. The POV shot is nothing more than an approximation of a character's vision. It is not an exact re-creation of that vision, for it does not resemble human vision in any physiological or subjective sense. If it did, it would not be stationary but would flit and jostle around; it would be interrupted by blinking eyelids, blurrings, spots, tears, and so on. In conventional filmmaking, the POV shot always ignores the physiology of vision. What happens instead is a sort of surrogate point of view, a shot that has the same vector as the character's line of sight but in reality is more like a camera on a tripod rather than the character's true vision. The POV shot is an abstract shot, an iconographic substitute for the character's vision. It pretends to be from the character's *point* of view, from a perspective, not verily through his or her own eyes, with all the blinks, blurs, and jiggles—not to mention raw subjectivity—that that would entail.

Another usage is the "masked POV" shot, often used to represent binocular vision (or vision through a telescope, camera, or keyhole). This shot is easy to notice: the edge of the frame is obfuscated with a curved, black masking. The masking acts as visual proof that the audience is seeing exactly what the character is seeing through his or her own eyes. These shots are generally very short takes. They serve simply to offer some piece of visual evidence to the viewer. But their relationship to the subjective shot is flimsy at best, for the cinema's binocular shot doesn't accurately capture what it looks like to peer through binoculars—in human vision, the two lens images tend to overlap and fuse into a single circle. Moreover, because real human vision does not come in a tidy, rectangular aspect ratio, one never actually notices the blackness at the edge of the image. The sideways figure-eight masking is simply the best that cinema can muster to approximate what binocular vision looks like. Cinema's binocular shot, then, is a type of icon for binocular vision, not an honest-to-goodness substitute for it.

The collection of visible evidence is often crucial in films, and the POV shot is commonly used to present to the audience evidence necessary to the film's narrative. The binocular shot is almost always used to convey some sort of visual fact to the viewer. Letters, telegrams, and notes are similar, as in *Casablanca* when Ilsa's good-bye note is pasted flat on the screen for the audience to read and then yanked back into diegetic space by a dusting of heavy raindrops. These shots are a holdover from the intertitles of the silent era. They walk the line between being a POV shot and being a subjective shot. Films like Antonioni's *Blow-Up*, Hitchcock's *Rear Window*, or Greenaway's *The Draughtsman's Contract* all rely on the collection and analysis of visible evidence. Further, one might also consider films focusing on audio evidence, such as De Palma's *Blow Out* or Coppola's *The Conversation*, or the subjective evidence of memory, as in Kurosawa's *Rashomon*, or even the evidentiary gaze of video games like *Ico*. As Grace Kelly says at the narrative crossroads of *Rear Window*, "Tell me everything you saw . . . and what you think it means."

But certain critical observations, like this one written in passing by Fredric Jameson, complicate the discussion so far on the POV shot:

"Point of view" in the strictest sense of seeing through a character's
eyes—as in Delmar Daves's *Dark Passage* [1947] or Robert Montgomery's *The Lady in the Lake* [1946]—has been a very marginal
narrative procedure indeed.[5]

Or as David Bordwell and his coauthors put it, very few films are
dominated by a single character's perspective, much less a character's
subjective perspective:

> If we take point-of-view to be an *optical* subjectivity, no classical
> film, not even the vaunted but misdescribed *Lady in the Lake* (1947),
> completely confines itself to what a character sees. If we regard a
> character's point-of-view as comprising what the character knows,
> we still find very few classical films that restrict themselves to this
> degree. . . . The classical film typically contains a few subjective
> point-of-view shots (usually of printed matter read by a character),
> but these are firmly anchored in an "objective" frame of reference.[6]

Let us consider in greater detail the type of POV shot that does pretend to emanate from the eyes of a particular character: the subjective shot. Like POV shots, subjective shots happen when two of the
looks, the look of the camera and the look of a single character, merge
together as one. Yet subjective shots are more extreme in their physiological mimicking of actual vision, for, as stated, they pretend to
peer outward from the eyes of an actual character rather than simply
to approximate a similar line of sight. Thus subjective shots are much
more volatile. They pitch and lurch. They get blinded by light or go
blurry. And within the diegesis, they elicit Willemen's "fourth look"
often, as other characters address the camera directly (in an attempt
to maintain the illusion that the camera is actually another character).
As Jameson writes, subjective shots are marginal, and I can see two
reasons why he would think so: they are materially marginalized in
that they happen relatively infrequently within the apparatus of filmmaking, and they are aesthetically marginalized in that they represent only specific moods and situations.

As both Jameson and Bordwell suggest, Robert Montgomery's noir
experiment *Lady in the Lake* is the most fully formed early example of
the subjective shot.[7] In this film, the camera becomes one with the
main character, Marlowe. Nearly every shot in the film is shot as if it

Lady in the Lake, directed by Robert Montgomery, 1947

were from the eyes of Marlowe. Thus the typical Hollywood conventions of shot/reverse shot, continuity editing, and so forth are shed to facilitate a new experimental convention, the merging of two "looks." The film attempts to move in real time—not true, we learn upon discovery of carefully hidden ellipses and cuts—but nevertheless, as Marlowe sees events in the world, the viewer sees them too. Images become evidence. (Indeed, the film eventually turns on a visual trick in which the viewer, as Marlowe, sees the cops approaching from a fire escape behind the crooked cop—a fact that the crooked cop is not willing to believe, since he is not privy to the special merging of looks afforded the viewer.)

Unfortunately the visual experiment of *Lady in the Lake* made identification problematic. Critics at the time called the subjective shot "gimmicky" and "flawed." Pascal Bonitzer called it "more tiring than fascinating."[8] (The early 1950s television cop show *The Plainclothesman* used the same conceit with slightly more success.) Each time Marlowe's body is also shown onscreen—in a mirror, when smoking, when crawling, being kissed, and so on—the illusion of the subjective shot is broken, and the viewer is reminded of the camera lens's failure to merge fully with Marlowe's own optics. The audience is thus trapped inside a sort of failed formal experiment, and the suturing together of the filmic apparatus begins to fray.

J. P. Telotte describes the detached, dreamlike quality of the film in which the viewer's avatar (Marlowe) both acts and sees itself acting:

> As the film opens, Marlowe is the sole object in the image field, as he comments upon the role of the detective. With our incarnation in his presence, through that pervasive subjective camera, he also becomes

that which is, after a fashion, "lost" for most of the narrative and thus the object of our own searching throughout the film, although most obviously when that absence is underscored by the many acknowledgements of Marlowe's presence, such as the mirror reflections or the guns aimed at his off-screen perspective. That enigmatic detachment, of course, as we both act and see ourselves in action, again typifies the dream experience.[9]

The same sense of detachment, claustrophobia, and nonidentification pervades the first hour of *Dark Passage* in which the main character, played by Humphrey Bogart, moves and talks in the first person, not unlike the technique used in *Lady in the Lake*. But the subjective perspective is only a ploy in this film, as the taxi scene demonstrates with Bogart's face deliberately bathed in shadow. The first section of the film is a cinematic conceit for not showing Bogart's presurgery face, and in that sense it is better motivated by the narrative than was Montgomery's film. But the subjective shots end after the plastic surgery, and the film returns to the shot conventions of classical Hollywood. It seems that only a scalpel can rid this film of the subjective camera angle.

While *Lady in the Lake* and *Dark Passage* are fascinating examples, they are not indicative of the vast majority of subjective shots used in the cinema. Edward Branigan is authoritative in this area. He contrasts the POV shot with the subjective shot (which he terms the "perception" shot), claiming that one is characterized by relative clarity, while the other is characterized by difficulty:

> In the case of character *sight*, what is important is not so much that a character sees something, but that he experiences difficulty *in seeing*. What is revealed is not the external object of a glance nor an internal state of the character, but a condition of sight itself. This feature of character vision is exploited in the perception [i.e., subjective] structure which differs from the POV structure in one important respect: In POV there is no indication of a character's mental condition—the character is only "present"—whereas in the perception [i.e., subjective] shot a signifier of mental condition has been *added* to an optical POV.[10]

Thus, to facilitate a deeper analysis of the subjective shot, there are two general observations worth mentioning. First, while POV shots are ubiquitous, subjective shots are much less common in narrative filmmaking. *Lady in the Lake* and *Dark Passage* notwithstanding, most narrative films don't include a single subjective shot, and in the films that do, there are generally only a handful of subjective shots used to achieve very specific results. Second, when a subjective shot is used, it generally signifies some type of negative vision. This is the "difficulty" that Branigan mentioned. It is sometimes an evil vision, or an in-human one, or simply a moment of alienation or detachment within a character. Few other shot styles are as closely associated with such a specifically defined mood. Yes, there are exceptions to these rules: for example, there is nothing inhuman or evil about Peter O'Toole's director's-eye shot of a bitten apple near the beginning of *The Stunt Man*, but the image is too quick to render much cinematic affect; likewise the use of the first person for a Steadicam shot at the start of *Wild Things* does little more than forecast the twists and turns of the film as a whole. Yet I hope to point out in what follows the largely alienating qualities of the vast majority of subjective shots in use in mainstream narrative film.

Mental Affect

One of the most common uses of the subjective shot is to show the optical perspective of a drugged, drowsy, drunk, or otherwise intoxicated character.[11] Samuel Fuller used this type of subjective shot in the opening sequence of *The Naked Kiss*. Here Kelly (Constance Towers) repeatedly strikes her inebriated male opponent. The combat is filmed from the opponent's subjective viewpoint looking back at her, and he is beaten down in a drunken stupor. The use of the subjective camera in this sequence is quite violent and unsettling, meant to convey not only the character's drunkenness but also the attacker's vitriol. The courtroom scene in *Sullivan's Travels* uses the subjective perspective in a similar fashion. In this scene, John Sullivan (Joel McCrea) has suffered a head injury and is delirious. The camera is shot in the first-person perspective, using filters to blur and obfuscate the shot. The technique is designed to mimic the character's traumatized subjective sensations. The camera's visual confusion approximates his own physiological trauma. In *Black Narcissus*, to cite another example, at the moment when Sister Ruth succumbs to her earthly passions, the camera cuts to a subjective shot that glows bright red. Then the camera

Notorious, directed by Alfred Hitchcock, 1946

careens to the floor, and the screen eclipses to a wash of royal blue after she faints. Her physiological state, intoxicated with passion, is conveyed to the viewer using the subjective shot. In still another example, from Hitchcock's *Notorious*, after Alicia is gradually subdued by a forced diet of narcotics, the sequence switches to a subjective camera, warping and blurring to depict her visual delirium. A similar shot is used in Alicia's drunk-driving scene; only then liquor and windblown hair obscure her vision instead of poison. In *Spellbound*, Hitchcock does the same: J. B.'s subjective shot through a glass of milk (which is spiked with bromide) exists purely to cantilever the character's physiognomy from psychotic trance to drug-induced slumber.

Detachment or Distancing

In the contemporary cinema, the film *Being John Malkovich* contains a wealth of subjective cinematography. Here the subjective shot does not repurpose the optical traits of intoxication but instead represents the feeling of disembodiment that would accompany leaving one's own body and entering the head of another person. (The film mimics a similar technique from the final vignette in *Everything You Always Wanted to Know About Sex* but Were Afraid to Ask* where a romantic liaison is observed through the eyes of a surrogate host.) The subjective shot effects the distortions of identity that would follow from such a radical physiological transformation. In the film, subjective shots are denoted by a binocular-like black oval mask that obfuscates the corners of the frame. Additionally the frequent use of a wide-angle lens adds a sense of vertigo to the shot. Since the narrative of the film revolves around the art of puppetry, the subjective shot is no doubt used here as a type of formal allegory for the inability to control one's actions, for being at the mercy of someone else. Just as in the uncomfortable lack of identification with the bodily movements of Marlowe's character in *Lady in the Lake*, the viewer of *Being John Malkovich* is thrown into an uneasy rapport with the diegesis of the film, which, one assumes, is precisely the point. If the subjective shot inhibited audience identification in the earlier film, it is leveraged here exactly because of its ability to alienate the viewer. The film demonstrates, essentially, that being in the first-person perspective is the same as being a puppet: the viewer is impotent and helpless, subject to the physical and psychological whims of the puppeteer. The short flashback of Elijah (the chimp), also shot using the subjective camera, underscores this point. Like a puppet, the infantile, feeble-minded chimp has little agency in this sequence, and thus the subjective shot fits him well. Being Malkovich is like being Elijah, or so the film's visual grammar would have one believe.

Other films have also used the subjective shot to portray a feeling of detachment or distancing. *Thomas in Love*—like *Lady in the Lake*, shot entirely with subjective camera—effects a sense of detachment, both literally in the portrayal of the main character's agoraphobia and also aesthetically with the rampant use of video monitor imagery. In *The Graduate*, when Ben Braddock (Dustin Hoffman) is paraded before his parents' friends in full scuba gear, the first-person subjective perspective is used to represent his feelings of impotence and alienation. The film's audio track is distinctly affected at this moment, and the mise-en-scène gives way to muted underwater colorings. This is not a typical way of seeing but instead an oppressive, decentering one. Likewise in *Risky Business* the subjective shot is used to emasculate the main character. It is used to show him at his point of least power, that is, when he is subject to the patronage of his parents. Some films carry this notion further. The opening shot of *The Insider* is a subjective shot masked by a gauze blindfold, designed to put the viewer in a state of uncertainty, even dread. When the son is hit by a car in *All about My Mother*, a subjective shot is used. Likewise Stanley Donen in *Charade* uses a subjective shot in the morgue scene near the film's beginning, placing the camera in the rather unnatural subjective viewpoint of a cadaver looking upward. The steel sarcophagus walls frame the shot on three sides, and this, coupled with a backward tracking movement, imparts a distinct sense of claustrophobia and helplessness to the viewer. Hitchcock has also used this mode effectively. In *Topaz*, when Juanita descends the stairway to confront the soldiers invading her residence, Hitchcock cuts to a quick, unsteady shot through her eyes to indicate that she is about to die. Then comes the most important shot of the film, a high overhead shot—a perspective perfected by Hitchcock, and one that no real human eye could ever attain—of her murdered body, the purple fabric of her dress flowing outward like a pool of blood. The two shots counterpoint each other: nothing but the alienating subjective shot on the stairs can prepare the viewer for the woeful murder shot. At that moment, Juanita's first-person vision is a dead vision. It invites dread and detachment into the scene.

What was detachment and alienation in *Topaz* was often flat-out terror in other Hitchcock films. In *The 39 Steps*, Hitchcock uses the subjective shot to transmit a sense of fear and foreboding when the news of Annabella's murder is first described aloud in the train compartment. In *Vertigo*, the famous filmic representation of acrophobia (a track-zoom shot looking straight down) is also a subjective shot. It is used to portray the intense fear and disorientation felt by someone suffering from vertigo. *The Blair Witch Project* does something similar, yet the fear of heights is replaced in this film by the fear of being lost. The film's interesting invention of a sort of "camcorder subjectivity," while not a subjective shot per se, nevertheless parallels the techniques of the subjective shot to heighten the sense of disorientation and fear.

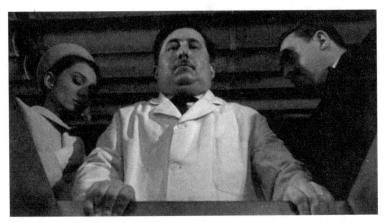

Charade, directed by Stanley Donen, 1963

Criminals and Monsters

Thus far, I have considered how the subjective shot is used to represent the first-person perspective of relatively average characters. They might be intoxicated, frightened, or otherwise out of joint, yet these characters are still human beings. However, these examples are not indicative of the majority of subjective shots in the cinema. The largest number of subjective shots represent the vision of aliens, criminals, monsters, or characters deemed otherwise inhuman by the film's narrative. Thus it should come as no surprise that the horror genre uses this convention relatively often. From early science-fiction monster films like *It Came from Outer Space*, to pioneering horror films like *Psycho* or *Halloween*, to the more recent film *The Eye*, the first-person subjective shot is used to show what Carol Clover calls "predatory" or "assaultive" vision, that is, a sadistic way of seeing characterized by aggressive action, forward movement, and onscreen violence. "*Predatory gazing* through the agency of the first-person camera," writes Clover, "is part of the stock-in-trade of horror."[12] *The Silence of the Lambs* is a good example of this type of predatory vision. The serial killer Buffalo Bill (aka Jame Gumb) dons night-vision goggles in the finale, and his subsequent subjective shots are used to present to the viewer the optics of raw criminality. The films *Jaws* and *Alien* both

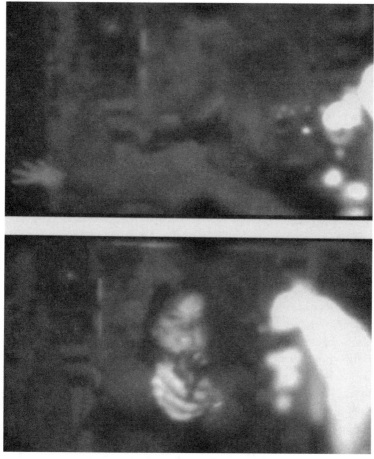

The Silence of the Lambs, directed by Jonathan Demme, 1991

use the subjective shot exclusively as the visual avatar for the killer monsters. In those films, the first-person perspective is a stalking, predatory vision, a killing vision. This way of seeing is also used often in slasher movies such as *Friday the 13th* (or, again, *Halloween*) to show the actual optical perspective of the killer. Brian De Palma, in *Casualties of War*, uses this perspective for a single scene in which an unknown assailant stalks another soldier and attempts to murder him with a grenade. De Palma used this technique again later in *Mission:*

Impossible, where the frequent use of first-person subjective shots during the first twenty minutes of the film is a sort of monstrous formal trauma that necessitates the systematic killing off of all of the film's leading characters, save one, before the film has even gotten under way. De Palma has used this technique before, too, as in the opening segment of *Blow Out*, where a knife-wielding murderer offers the viewer his own first-person perspective as a psychopath. As in *Lady in the Lake*, De Palma uses a mirror to show the audience a reflection of the first-person character looking at himself. In both films it is a peculiar moment. Since this way of seeing is so alienating in narrative filmmaking, viewers are not altogether comfortable looking in the first person, much less witnessing themselves in a mirror looking in the first person.

The intersection of the POV shot and the subjective shot is illustrated nicely by Hitchcock's *Rear Window*. As others have pointed out, the film overflows with POV shots, and indeed the entire narrative thrust of the film, along with its poetic import, revolves around the various layers of watching, being watched, seeing, and identifying.[13] So while POV shots are crucial in the film, subjective shots are also used in certain instances, as in the soft-focus filmic portrait of Kelly upon her entrance. The shot is neither predatory nor monstrous, but it does have a confusing, dreamlike quality, attesting to Jeffries's psychological state at the time. When the subjective shot does turn monstrous, in the climactic scene near the end of the film, it is used to illustrate the temporary blindness of the killer after each flashbulb burst. Blindness is depicted by using a bright red circle that overtakes the frame. This is literally the optical perspective of the salesman, a killer whose way of seeing at that moment is no less bloodthirsty than the shark camera in *Jaws* or the night-vision camera in *The Silence of the Lambs*. A simple POV shot would not go red, for it does not pretend to mimic actual vision. This shot *must* be a subjective shot, for the viewer is designed to see, in a physiological sense, exactly what the killer sees. There is nothing sinister about a POV shot (dozens of POV shots come and go during the film with little fanfare), but subjective shots signify something dark and murderous, and so when Hitchcock elects to use a subjective shot, he comes up with a formally affected image, emanating from the eyes of a murderer.

In this sense, it is easy to see how the subjective shot is a close cousin of the snuff film, connected as they are through the coupling of predatory vision and the impotence of the gaze. *Peeping Tom* probably illustrates this best, imbricating the necessarily impotent physical positioning of the viewer with the onscreen events through the use of the subjective shot. *The Eyes of Laura Mars* or the newer *Strange Days* do something similar. During one of *Strange Days*'s first-person frolics, Lenny (Ralph Fiennes) reveals himself in a mirror while maintaining the first-person perspective (with a cheat away allowed for Bigelow's camera to stay hidden). Faith (Juliette Lewis) asks, "You wanna watch? Or are you gonna do?" The question casts doubt on the ability of the subjective gaze to do anything. It casts doubt on the viewer as well as the audience, for both parties know that the subjective shots in the film are doomed to fail at *doing* and are instead resigned to an impotent form of camcorder playback sans joystick, which of course is the best the cinema can muster.

Computers

As discussed thus far, subjective shots are often paired with intoxicated humans and bloodthirsty monsters. But perhaps the most successful use of the subjective shot is when it is used to represent computerized, cybernetic, or machinic vision (or when, as in the case of "smart bomb" video targeting footage, it *is* machinic vision). In *The Terminator,* to underscore the computerized artificiality of his cyborg's visual cortex, James Cameron includes four shots where the Terminator's eyes and the camera lens merge. The first, after a violent shoot-out in the "TechNoir" nightclub, is seen as a degraded orange-on-black image. The Terminator's visual field is overlaid with target crosshairs and lines of computer data. The shot is short, uncoupling the camera's eye and the Terminator's "I" after only a few seconds. At three other moments in the film (the attack on the police precinct, the barking dog at Reese and Connor's motel hideout, and the penultimate tanker trunk scene), Cameron uses the same visual style to designate a merging of looks. Computer readouts, diagrams, graphics, flashing cursors, and scrolling texts are all used to give the Terminator's image a computer-like patina. (The patina overlay pops up in other films too, as in the case of the computer HAL in *2001,* whose digital vision is deeply affected via the use of a wide-angle lens, or as in *Lost Highway*, where the dozen or so subjective shots that do exist are presented to the viewer via the lens of a security camera, thereby adopting the grainy, low-res image quality of amateur video. The video patina acts as a buffer to mediate the shock of the subjective shot.)

During the repairs scene in the cyborg's hotel hideout, the source of the Terminator's visual patina is revealed: he has robotic eyes, complete with lens, aperture, and recording mechanism. The Terminator's visual apparatus, then, is quite similar to the film's apparatus in which it is contained. Merging the two looks makes sense when it is machine on machine. It goes with the grain. Hence, when the Terminator is finally killed and his glowing red eye fades and dies, the film must also end, having finally lost its ability to merge the camera lens with the character eye.

Full of clear allusions to its cyborg sci-fi predecessor, *Robocop* perfects the art of mixing filmic looks begun in *The Terminator*. Willemen's fourth look is employed early in the film through the use of newscast footage and commercials. Robocop is a machine, but since his bodily core is human (resuscitated from Alex Murphy, the cop), the merging of film body and character body must be delicately navigated. Murphy must first be obliterated as a body—that is, *dehumanized*—before the viewer is allowed to see through his eyes. Obliteration comes in the form of firepower. His hand is blown off; he is pelted with dozens of rounds; and then he is shot through the head at point-blank range and left for dead. As he is taken to the hospital, the camera eye and Murphy's ego perspective merge for the first time. His eye is shown in close-up. But he dies, and the image dies too; the film goes dark for several seconds.

As the image wakes up, the movie camera *is* Robocop. Video is used rather than film, and the image is filtered to mimic Robocop's computerized vision: the vertical hold of the image is lost temporarily, static degrades the image, and text flickers across the screen. As a technician orders, "Bring in the LED!" the viewer witnesses a computerized grid superimposed over the frame. The same technician later kisses Robocop's visor, leaving a blurry red mark on the screen. (The visor kiss is more plausible here than the same kiss scene in *Lady in the Lake* simply because Robocop's visual apparatus already contains a

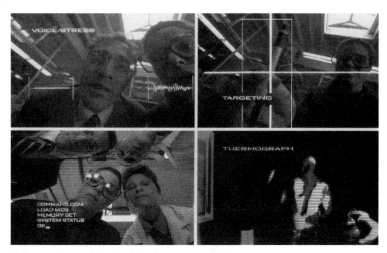

Robocop, directed by Paul Verhoeven, 1987

glass screen, the visor, whereas Marlowe's visual apparatus does not.) These are all instances of the subjective shot, and they all signify computer vision.

As the narrative of the film dwells on his rise in popularity as a law-enforcement machine, Robocop's subjective vision becomes more and more important to the film. In the hostage scene at City Hall, the conventional cinematography is interrupted by Robocop's "Thermograph" vision, a type of computer vision used to see through walls. Robocop's normal robotic vision is mediated further as heat-sensitive shapes are mixed with the already degraded video image.

John McTiernan's *Predator* uses a similar "thermographic" effect to designate the merging of the camera lens with the Predator's optics. At key moments in *Predator*, the viewer sees a colorized, heat-sensitive image that is meant to be the Predator's actual vision. In this sense, the formal rules of the subjective shot in *Predator* are quite similar to *Jaws* and *Alien*; only in McTiernan's film the monster's predatory vision is augmented by a computer.

What might appear here as a savvy demystification of the filmic apparatus in *Predator* or *Robocop* is in fact a reinscription of a sense of optical exactitude for the subjective positions of the two title characters. The viewer is not unsatisfied by seeing the visible, computer-enhanced traces of Robocop's vision because these traces—the low-resolution video image, degraded with static and computer effects—reinforce the very fantasy of cyborg vision. Being cybernetic, then, provides a necessary alibi for the affect of the first-person perspective. After all, Robocop's vision (like the Terminator's) *is* robotic, while Marlowe's was nothing of the sort. *Lady in the Lake* fails not because it doesn't get it right but because it doesn't get it wrong enough. It tried to merge the camera body with a real, human body, a dubious proposition in the cinema, whereas in films like *Robocop* or *The Terminator* the camera merges with an *artificial* body, one that is more similar to the machinic apparatus of film itself, and likewise of digital media. An affinity based in prosthetics, mechanics, and visuality bonds the camera together with the figure of the cyborg eye. These films mark one aspect of the aesthetic transition from cinema to digital media and hence to video gaming.

As these many examples illustrate, the first-person subjective perspective is used in film primarily to effect a sense of alienation, otherness, detachment, or fear. Further, more often than not, this type of shot is used to show the vision of criminals, monsters, or killer machines. This analysis shows that the merging of camera and character in the subjective shot is more successful if the character in question is marked as computerized in some way. The first-person subjective perspective must be instigated by a character who is already mediated through some type of informatic artifice. Necessary for this effect are all the traces of computer image processing: scan lines, data printouts, target crosshairs, the low resolution of video, feedback, and so on. In other words, a deviation from the classical model of representation is necessary via the use of technological manipulation of the image—a technological patina.

Action as Image

So far I have considered a specific and somewhat rare type of shot used in narrative filmmaking, the subjective shot. But let me make this discussion slightly more specific, first by making reference to a different medium altogether, the video game, and second by adding

Spellbound, directed by Alfred Hitchcock, 1945

another piece of visual iconography to the frame, a weapon. Video games are wildly diverse in their formal grammar, but in the specific gaming genre known as the first-person shooter (FPS), a gaming genre invented in the 1970s and perfected by Id Software in the early 1990s with games like *Wolfenstein 3D* and *Doom*, there are several formal conventions that appear over and over. First, FPS games are played in the subjective, or first-person, perspective and therefore are the visual progeny of subjective camera techniques in the cinema. But perhaps equally essential to the FPS genre is the player's *weapon*, which generally appears in the right foreground of the frame. While a more detailed analysis would certainly include other elements such as the heads-up display, for simplicity's sake let me claim that these two elements alone—a subjective camera perspective, coupled with a weapon in the foreground—constitute the kernel of the image in the FPS genre. (Let me also underscore that the analysis of gamic visuality in this section is relevant only to first-person, and to a certain extent third-person, shooter games. An entirely different theory of visuality would need to be developed for RTS games, turn-based

Half-Life, Valve Software, 1998

RPGs, and other genres, something I attempt, however tangentially, and admittedly [but deliberately] without much reference to the visual cortex at all, in chapter 4.)

Perhaps not surprisingly, even the precise visual idiom of the FPS video game appears decades before in the cinema. In 1925, for example, Buster Keaton used a prototypical FPS shot in the film *Go West.* As in *Jaws,* the perspective comes from the point of view of a predatory animal. In Keaton's case, the animal is a stampeding bull, and the bull's horns are the weapon that appears hovering in the foreground of the shot. While the shot is technically in a third-person (bovine) perspective—the camera is mounted on the head of the bull, not where its eyes would be—the generic conventions are all there: an affective ego perspective, with a weapon in the foreground. Other examples appear here and there in the early history of cinema.

So while video games are responsible for mainstreaming the FPS shot, it is clear that the shot itself was invented in the cinema. Twenty years after the Keaton film, Hitchcock presented a fully articulated FPS shot in the finale of his film *Spellbound.* Following a complex set of movements, the shot begins in FPS perspective as a gun is trained

Go West, directed by Buster Keaton, 1925

on Constance Petersen (Ingrid Bergman). Then the gun is turned back onto the camera, and in a brutal reworking of Willemen's "fourth look," as well as an allusion to the famous final shot of *The Great Train Robbery,* the subjective character fires back at the subjective camera. It is suicide for the character and for the image (the masochism suggested by Clover). Hitchcock punctuates the bullet's explosion with a full-screen flash of red color in this otherwise black-and-white movie. Earlier, during the film's famous dream sequence, an enigmatic deck of cards serves as a prop in a second, much shorter, subjective shot. And in a brief flashback, when Anthony Edwardes (Gregory Peck) recalls how he killed his brother as a youth, another FPS shot is used to show the fatal accident. All three uses of the subjective shooter perspective serve to heighten specific emotions in the viewer: confusion during the dream sequence, trauma during the death sequence, and shock during the finale. The shots form a trio of grief: first affective, then expressive, and finally reflexive. In this sense, the FPS perspective is the visual pivot for all of Hitchcock's suspense in the film. And he would flirt with the FPS again in a later film, using an FPS shot in the duel at the end of *Topaz* (an alternate ending

Topaz, directed by Alfred Hitchcock, 1969

that, due to preview audience dislike, was banished and replaced with milder fare in the theatrical release).

The real-time, over-the-shoulder tracking shots of Gus Van Sant's *Elephant* evoke third-person shooter games like *Max Payne*, a close cousin of the FPS. Then the film shifts into a proper FPS perspective at a few crucial moments to depict actual gun violence. Additionally, the film uses a boxy 1:33 frame shape, rather than the wide aspect ratio often used in feature films, to reference the boxy shape of television monitors and the console game systems that rely on them. That the 1999 Columbine massacre was blamed on such games remains present but unexamined in this taut, pensive film. Van Sant is clearly cognizant of the visual idiom of gaming, as illustrated in the campfire monologue on a fictional, *Civilization*-like game in his earlier film *Gerry*, a filmic landscape that reappears as a game called "GerryCount" played on a laptop in *Elephant*. "In *Elephant*, one of the killers is briefly playing a video game," explains Van Sant. "We couldn't get rights to *Doom* so we designed one ourselves that resembles *Gerry*, with two guys walking in a desert."[14] Additionally Van Sant used a first-person subjective shot during the penultimate sequence of his *Psycho* remake. While there is no expressed allusion to gaming, the quick shot illustrates the paralysis of the first person in film as Norman Bates reels inside of mental disorientation and confinement in the hands of the law and his mother's psychic grip. The shot is not in Hitchcock's

Elephant, directed by Gus Van Sant, 2003

Elephant

original, suggesting that our general regime of vision has changed subtly in the decades since the earlier film—decades coinciding exactly with the invention and development of video gaming as a medium. A few dozen other FPS shots appear here and there in other films. My unscientific survey recorded the following instances: midway through *Goodfellas*, a gun is trained on Ray Liotta's character in a subjective shot as he lies in bed; an FPS shot appears at the forty-eight-minute mark of *High Plains Drifter*; *Aguirre: The Wrath of God* and *Damn the Defiant!* both have FPS shots, using a cannon as the foreground weapon; *Treasure Island* (1950) contains an FPS rifle shot; *What's Up, Doc?* contains an FPS pistol shot; *Magnum Force* contains a series of FPS pistol shots; the night-vision sequence at the end of *The Silence of the Lambs* also shifts into the idiom of the first-person shooter for a brief second as the killer draws a bead on his would-be victim.

Gamic Vision

We have seen how filmmaking predates and predicts certain visual styles that would later become central for first-person shooter video games. Yet game design is also influencing filmmaking in certain fundamental ways, as well as deviating from it. Neo's training scenes in *The Matrix* mimic the training levels that commonly appear at the opening of many games. These training levels can be incorporated into the narrative of the game (*Metroid Prime*) or disconnected from the narrative of the game (*Half-Life*). They simply allow the gamer to become familiar with the controller and learn basic game rules. Neo must do the same before he plunges headlong into the Matrix for real. But beyond the transfection of gamic conventions into film *narrative*, there also exist several instances, in this movie and others, where specific formal innovations from games have migrated into the formal grammar of filmmaking. This could be called a *gamic cinema*.

The subjective shot is not just about seeing, as Steven Shaviro explains, but rather primarily about motion through space. He writes on the subjective shots in *Strange Days*:

> Events unfold in real time, in a single take, from a single point of
> view. These sequences are tactile, or haptic, more than they are

visual. The subjective camera doesn't just look at a scene. It moves actively through space. It gets jostled, it stops and starts, it pans and tilts, it lurches forward and back. It follows the rhythms of the whole body, not just that of the eyes. This is a presubjective, affective and not cognitive, regime of vision.[15]

What video games teach cinema is that the camera can be subjective with regard to a specific character, as I have already discussed, but further *that the camera can be subjective with regard to computerized space.* If computers have a gaze of their own, it is this. Is "bullet time" in *The Matrix* a subjective shot? Certainly not, using the traditional definition of the subjective shot by Bordwell et al. But if one considers the "gaze" of the three-dimensional rendering technology itself as it captures and plots physical spaces in Euclidean geometry, which is nothing but an avatar for the first-person perspective of the viewer or gamer, then the answer is certainly yes. To this extent, I agree with Vivian Sobchack when she writes that "electronic presence has neither a point of view nor a visual situation, such as we experience, respectively, with the photograph and the cinema."[16] Or as Manovich claims: computerized visuality, while still a way of seeing, is no longer about *light* but is instead about space. The traditional cinematic POV has fallen away, and an electronic one has taken its place. In other words, shooter games (and the digital apparatus behind them) have expanded the definitional bounds of the subjective shot. The reason is that, with FPS games, the first-person subjective perspective is so omnipresent and so central to the grammar of the entire game that it essentially becomes coterminous with it. This is what Shaviro means by the term "affective regime of vision." FPS games use almost nothing else, and this regime of vision is seeping back into filmmaking as movies become more and more digital.

This point can be summarized in an initial claim: *gamic vision requires fully rendered, actionable space.* Traditional filmmaking almost never requires the construction of full spaces. Set designers and carpenters build only the portion of the set that will appear within the frame. Because a director has complete control over what does appear within the frame, this task is easy to accomplish. The camera positions are known in advance. Once the film is complete, no new camera positions will ever be included. (Even a film shot on location will use a specific subset of the spatial environment. Only in special cases, as in the 360-degree pan shot at the start of *Cobra Verde* or in the twirling sets in films like *Lola Montes*, is a full landscape ever captured on film. But even then the spatial environment is *recorded*, not rendered, and can never be repenetrated, zoomed, moved, or reinitialized as is doable in a three-dimensional model.) The fascinating "100 cameras" video technique used by Lars von Trier in *Dancer in the Dark*, whereby dozens of small cameras are embedded in the shooting location to record, in parallel, an entire scene from all angles simultaneously, is an ingenious approximation of digital rendering; yet despite its unique polyvisuality, the technique remains essentially a throwback to older cinematic conventions of distinct shots sewn together via montage. By contrast, game design explicitly requires the construction of a complete space in advance that is then exhaustively explorable without montage. In a shooter, because the game designer cannot restrict the movement of the gamer, the complete play space must be rendered three-dimensionally in advance. The camera position in many games is not restricted. The player is the one who controls the camera position, by looking, by moving, by scrolling, and so on. Jay Bolter and Richard Grusin put the matter quite clearly when they contrast a film like *Lady in the Lake* with the game *Myst*:

> *Myst* is an interactive detective film in which the player is cast in the role of detective. It is also a film "shot" entirely in the first person, in itself a remediation of the Hollywood style, where first-person point of view is used only sparingly—except in special cases, such as *Strange Days* recently and some film noir in the 1940s. . . . Like many of the other role-playing games, *Myst* is in effect claiming that it can succeed where film noir failed: that it can constitute the player as an active participant in the visual scene.[17]

So fifty years later, the failed experiment of *Lady in the Lake* has finally found some success, only it required the transmigration from one medium to another entirely.

A corollary of my previous claim about actionable space is that gaming *makes montage more and more superfluous*. The montage technique, perfected by the cinema, has diminished greatly in the aesthetic shift into the medium of gaming. The cinematic interludes that appear as cut scenes in many games do indeed incorporate montage, but gameplay itself is mostly edit free. Counterexamples include cutting between various visual modes: opening the map in *World of Warcraft*; the use of a sniper rifle or night-vision goggles; cutting between different camera positions, as with looking in the rearview mirror in driving games like *True Crime*. A game like *Manhunt* uses montage, but only when it explicitly copies the conventions of video. So while there may exist montage between different modes of the game, there is little montage inside the distinct modes of gameplay. In this sense, the preponderance of continuous-shot filmmaking today (*Timecode*, *Russian Ark*) is essentially a sublimation of the absence of montage in digital poetics (i.e., not the increased availability of long-format recording techniques, as the technological determinists would lead one to believe). Game designers never had to stop and change reels (as Hitchcock had to in *Rope*), yet they still marginalized montage from the beginning, removing it from the core formal grammar of video games. Ingenious tricks are used instead, as in a game like *Metroid Prime*, where the transition from third person to first person is accomplished not with an edit but with a swooping fly-through shot where the camera, in third person, curves around to the rear of the player character and then tracks forward, swiftly passing through the back of the cranium to fuse instantly the first-person optics of the character with the first-person optics of the player. Tricks like this help attain a level of fluidity not seen in previous visual media like film or television. Abandoning montage creates the conditions of possibility for the first-person perspective in games. The lack of montage is necessary for the first-person way of seeing, even if the game itself is a side-scroller, or a top-view shooter, or otherwise *not* rendered in the first person. Where film montage is fractured and discontinuous, gameplay is fluid and continuous. Hence the gamic way of seeing is similar to human vision in ways that film, and television and video, for that matter, never were.

Following from the first two claims, one can observe that in gamic vision *time and space are mutable within the diegesis in ways unavailable before*. Games have the luxury of being able to exist outside real, optical time. Games pause, speed up, slow down, and restart often. But more than that, they can also transpire in moments of suspended

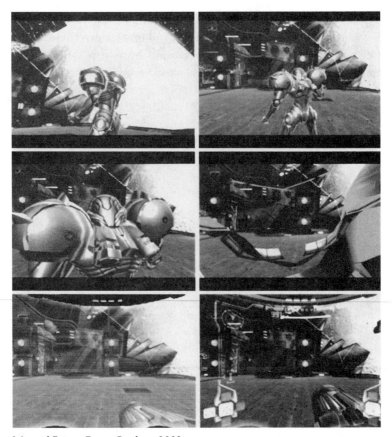

Metroid Prime, Retro Studios, 2002

time, as in turn-based role-playing games (RPGs) where the player plays (sets up actions, inspects statistics, rearranges character formations) solely during the *interstices* between other actions. Film has never had this luxury. Films are time based and must transpire through time in order to be played, to be experienced. Thus "bullet time" in *The Matrix* is one of those rare moments of cinematic illusion where the digital aesthetics of gaming actually penetrate and influence the aesthetic of the film. During bullet time, the time of the action is slowed or stopped, while the time of the film continues to proceed. As the film continues moving at speed, the action onscreen is artificially retarded into what Jameson calls "the great leaps and somersaults of these henceforth supernatural bodies across space itself."[18] This is something that, traditionally, only video games (or any medium using computer-driven, three-dimensional models) have been able to do, not classical cinema. Thus it might make sense to think of bullet time as a brief moment of gamic cinema, a brief moment where the aesthetic of gaming moves in and takes over the film, only to disappear seconds later. Of course, the poetic irony of bullet time is that technologically it relies on an older medium, still photography, rather than a newer one; an amateur could reproduce the special effect using an arc of a few dozen still cameras, a film camera on each end of the arc, and a cutting suite. The use of a series of still-photographic cameras is merely the technological trick that produces the synchronic illusion of a three-dimensionally rendered physical space.

As in *The Matrix* series, the "virtual" is often used as a sort of narrative camouflage applied to films to explain why time and space have suddenly become so mutable. This is illustrated by the rash of films in recent years dwelling on the difference between the so-called real world and an imaginary world existing in parallel to it (*Fight Club*, *The Sixth Sense*, *The Others*, and so on). Quite often the plots turn on the inability to distinguish one from the other. Particularly striking examples include *Strange Days* and Tarsem Singh's singular effort *The Cell*. The techniques of digital cinema made it possible to realize more fully the aesthetic vision of virtuality, in ways that were more difficult in the past. With the preponderance of digital cinema techniques in Singh (and we can only assume in Bigelow as well), game-like moments exist throughout both films. As discussed, the subjective shots in *Strange Days* are directly connected to FPS games. But *The Cell* goes the route of *The Matrix* instead, as illustrated in the "Pantheon dive" where Catherine falls downward through space and is arrested midair in a slow-motion, waterlike gesture. This approximates part of the visual technique in "bullet time," and it is a technique that has been repeated many times over in everything from car commercials to music videos.

A final claim is that the new influence of gaming *elevates the status of artificiality as an aesthetic*. Cronenberg's *eXistenZ*, which couldn't be more different from *The Matrix*, is remarkable for its ability to eschew computer graphics and digital processing, yet still capture some of gaming's specific qualities. Unlike *The Matrix*, where the inclusion of gaming is accomplished via visual effects, Cronenberg's film alludes to gaming in its mise-en-scène, particularly in the film's staging of action and dialogue. The conceit of the film is that all the action transpires inside a game, which the viewer is led to believe is also titled "eXistenZ." But then one learns that this might also be a game-within-a-game with the real world somewhere yet outside of it, the discernment of which is not clear, leaving the film characters in some final spiral of psychosis. Yes, the narrative of the film is about gaming, but it is the stilted dialogue and deliberately affected filmmaking in *eXistenZ* that is gamelike. Turn-based games such as RPGs have a different way of pacing and presenting dialogue. The rhythm of language is unique in this type of game. Language is transactional. It is repeated in simple branching, or hypertextual, structures. Language is often more utilitarian than narrative oriented. Game interludes often exist to give clues to the players for what they must do next. Often these written or spoken clues are then excerpted and repeated as briefs or strategy notes for the gamers to consult as they play the level. In games, language is used to relay facts or to summarize scores and statistics. The language in *eXistenZ* follows a game logic for dialogue rather than a film logic. The stilted dialogue that permeates many of the scenes references the way that textual and spoken dialogue is delivered in games. The film often repeats canned dialogue, both within the diegesis of the "eXistenZ" game when incidental characters fall into holding patterns and must be addressed by name and prompted for their queues in the game to continue talking, but also outside the game (which might be a game too; one does not know), as when several characters repeat the phrase "eXistenZ by Antenna . . . eXistenZ by Antenna" in the same machinelike monotone. "These *eXistenZ* characters are parodies of computer generated characters," writes Eddo Stern. They follow "autistic conversational algorithms."[19]

To end, let me restate that the subjective optical perspective is one of the least common ways of seeing in narrative film. The subjective camera is largely marginalized in filmmaking and used primarily to effect a sense of alienated, disoriented, or predatory vision. Yet with the advent of video games, a new set of possibilities were opened up for the subjective shot. In games the first-person perspective is not marginalized but instead is commonly used to achieve an intuitive sense of affective motion. It is but one of the many ways in which video games represent action. In other words, video games are the first mass media to effectively employ the first-person subjective perspective, whereas film uses it only for special occasions. Certainly some of the same violence of the filmic first person lingers, and hence many FPS games—*Quake, America's Army, Half-Life,* and on and on— involve large amounts of killing. But at the same time, many shooters, like *Metal Gear Solid* or *Thief,* require the player to *avoid* violence as much as confront it. Plus, game violence is just as common in non-first-person games. So I argue that it is the affective, active, mobile quality of the first-person perspective that is key for gaming, not its violence. Unlike film before it, in gaming there is no simple connection to be made between the first-person perspective and violent vision. What was predatory vision in the cinema is now simply "active" vision. As far as identification is concerned, film failed with the subjective shot, but where film failed, games succeed (due primarily to the fact that games have controllers and require player action). Where film uses the subjective shot to represent a problem with identification, games use the subjective shot to *create* identification. While film has thus far used the subjective shot as a corrective to break through and destroy certain stabilizing elements in the film apparatus, games use the subjective shot to facilitate an active subject position that enables and facilitates the gamic apparatus.

3

Social Realism

On March 21, 2003, a day into the second Iraq war, Sony filed a trademark application for the phrase "shock and awe," apparently for future use as a PlayStation game title. The phrase, and the American military strategy it describes, was in fact not such an unlikely candidate for the PlayStation. The console system has long flirted with game formats based in realistic scenarios, from Sony's own *SOCOM: U.S. Navy Seals* to Electronic Arts' *Madden NFL*. A month later, responding to criticism, Sony dropped the application, stating they did not intend to use the expression "shock and awe" in any upcoming games. But they have not dropped their fetish for realistic gaming scenarios. Indeed, reality is thriving today in many types of media, particularly gaming, where the polygon count continues to go up and up, or in cinema with the Wachowski brothers continuing to ruminate on the nature of "the real" (via Zizek, via Baudrillard, and back to Lacan, one presumes), or in television in the form of reality TV.

The conventional wisdom on realism in gaming is that, because life today is so computer mediated, gamers actually benefit from hours of realistic gameplay. The time spent playing games trains the gamer to be close to the machine, to be quick and responsive, to understand interfaces, to be familiar with simulated worlds. This was Ronald Reagan's argument in the 1980s when he famously predicted that action video games were training a new generation of cyber-warriors ready to fight real foes on the real battlefield (itself computer enhanced). Today it is evident that he was right: flight simulators, *Doom*, and now *America's Army* are all realistic training tools at some level, be they skill builders in a utilitarian sense or simply instructive of a larger militaristic ideology.[1]

In scholarship thus far the discourse on realism in gaming has been limited mainly to talk of screen violence and its supposed deleterious effects on gamers. This talk has grown so loud that I can't help conjure up various equations and feedback loops tallying doses of violent intake measured against the gamer's future evildoing. Call this the "Columbine theory" of realism in gaming: games plus gore equals psychotic behavior, and around and around. The Columbine theory is not the only interesting debate, however, and, granting it due significance to social scientists and the like, I will politely sidestep it here and return to the debates around realism as cultural critics have engaged them to date in other media.

One of the central theoretical issues in video gaming is how and in what way one can make connections between the gaming world and the real world, both from the inside outward in the form of affective action, and from the outside inward in the form of realistic modeling. In previous theories of visual culture, this is generally referred to as the problematic of representation. But in gaming the concept of representation's does not account for the full spectrum of issues at play. Representation refers to the creation of meaning about the world through images. So far, debates about representation have focused on whether images (or language, or what have you) are a faithful, mimetic mirror of reality thereby offering some unmediated truth about the world, or conversely whether images are a separate, constructed medium thereby standing apart from the world in a separate semantic zone. Games inherit this same debate. But because games are not merely watched but played, they supplement this debate with the phenomenon of action. It is no longer sufficient to talk about the visual or textual representation of meaning. Instead the game theorist must talk about actions, and the physical or game worlds in which they transpire. One might call this a problematic of "correspondences" (rather than just "representation"), for thinking about correspondences lets one consider the kinetic, affective, and material dimensions in debates around meaning and representation.[2] One is prompted to return to Aristotle's notion of mimesis in the *Poetics*. And indeed this is crucial. But as Johan Huizinga reminded us many years ago in his writings on play, "It is *methectic* rather than *mimetic*."[3]

"Realisticness" versus Social Realism

In this chapter, I would like to describe how traditional theories of realism can be applied to video games, and then propose an expansion of the concept of realism to include new problems that games present.

Within the world of gaming, it is possible to divide games into two piles: those that have as their central conceit the mimetic reconstruction of real life, and those resigned to fantasy worlds of various kinds. Thus, SOCOM is about the real Navy Seals, *The Sims Hot Date* is about real dating (one assumes), and *Madden NFL* is about the real National Football League, while games like *Final Fantasy*, *Grand Theft Auto*, and *Unreal Tournament* transpire in fictional worlds with fictional characters and fictional narratives. Thus games are generally either realistic or fantastical. Expressing the perspective of game designers, Bruce Shelley writes that realism is a sort of tool that can be leveraged for greater effect in gameplay but is ultimately noncrucial: "Realism and historical information are resources or props we use to add interest, story, and character to the problems we are posing for the player. That is not to say that realism and historic fact have no importance, they are just not the highest priority."[4]

But realistic narrative and realistic representation are two different things. So these two piles start to blur. For instance, listening to music, ordering pizza, and so on in *The Sims* is most probably closer to the narratives of normal life than is storming an enemy base in SOCOM, despite the fact that the actual visual imagery in SOCOM is more realistically rendered than the simplistic avatars, isometric perspective, and nondiegetic wall cutaways in *The Sims*. Likewise *Unreal Tournament 2003* has a more photorealistic graphics engine than *Grand Theft Auto III*, but the former narrative is sci-fi fluff at best, leaving it at a loss for realism. During the Cold War, games like *Missile Command* presented a protorealist anxiety narrative about living under the threat of nuclear annihilation, yet the game's interface remained highly unrealistic and abstract. The infamous 1988 game *NARC* presented a realist window on urban blight by depicting police violence and drug dealers, couching its gory imagery in an anti-drug stance. John Dell's text simulation *Drug Wars* (1984) did something similar, explaining the drug trade through the economics of the market—buy low, sell high. Atari's *BattleZone*, one of the first games to feature a truly interactive three-dimensional environment, was deemed so realistic by the U.S. military that they hired Atari to build a special version used to train tank pilots. Yet the game's vector graphics are too sparse and abstract to qualify as truly realist.

If these games are any indication, it would seem that gaming is a purely expressionistic medium with no grounding in realism no matter how high the polygon counts or dots per inch, or perhaps that gaming is one of those media wherein an immense chasm stands between empirical reality and its representation in art.

But this is something of a straw man, for realisticness and realism are most certainly not the same thing. If they were the same, realism in gaming would simply be a mathematical process of counting the polygons and tracing the correspondences. Realisticness is a yardstick held up to representation. And so at the level of representation, *SOCOM* is no different from other games based in real life. That is to say, at the level of representation, it is a realistic game, just as *Tony Hawks Pro Skater 4* is realistic when it lets the gamer actually skate, albeit virtually, at the real Kona skatepark in Jacksonville, Florida. Realisticness is important, to be sure, but the more realisticness takes hold in gaming, the more removed from gaming it actually becomes, relegated instead to simulation or modeling. This is a contradiction articulated well by Fredric Jameson in his essay "The Existence of Italy":

"Realism" is, however, a particularly unstable concept owing to its simultaneous, yet incompatible, aesthetic and epistemological claims, as the two terms of the slogan, "representation of reality," suggest.

These two claims then seem contradictory: the emphasis on this or that type of truth content will clearly be undermined by any intensified awareness of the technical means or representational artifice of the work itself. Meanwhile, the attempt to reinforce and to shore up the epistemological vocation of the work generally involves the suppression of the formal properties of the realistic "text" and promotes an increasingly naive and unmediated or reflective conception of aesthetic construction and reception. Thus, where the epistemological claim succeeds, it fails; and if realism validates its claim to being a correct or true representation of the world, it thereby ceases to be an *aesthetic* mode of representation and falls out of art altogether. If, on the other hand, the artistic devices and technological equipment whereby it captures that truth of the world are explored and stressed and foregrounded, "realism" will stand unmasked as a mere reality- or realism-*effect*, the reality it purported to deconceal falling at once into the sheerest representation and illusion. Yet no viable conception of realism is possible unless both these demands or claims are honored simultaneously, prolonging and preserving—rather than "resolving"—this constitutive tension and incommensurability.[5]

When one thinks solely in terms of realisticness—Jameson's "naive and unmediated or reflective conception of aesthetic construction"— one detracts from a larger understanding of realism. Put another way: realisticness and realism are two very different things.

André Bazin defined realism in the cinema as a technique to approximate the basic phenomenological qualities of the real world. And he knew well that "phenomenological qualities" did not simply mean realistic visual representation. It also means real life in all its dirty details, hopeful desires, and abysmal defeats. Because of this, realism often arrives in the guise of social critique. Realism in the cinema, dubbed "neorealism" at the time to distinguish it historically from its predecessors in literature and fine art, is defined by several formal techniques. These include the use of nonprofessional actors, the absence of histrionics, real-life scenery, amateur cinematography, grainy film stock, long takes, and minimal editing. But further, Bazin also associated neorealism with a certain type of *narrative*, not simply a certain type of form. So while Bazin acknowledges the formal tendencies of realism (long takes, amateur actors, and so on), and even praises the mise-en-scène of filmmakers like Vittorio de Sica, he writes that "we would define as 'realist,' then, all *narrative* means tending to bring an added measure of reality to the screen."[6] Thus it is the story of the unemployed father that ultimately constitutes the realist core of de Sica's *The Bicycle Thief*, not its degraded style. Jameson follows this by reinforcing what Bazin knew to be obvious, that neorealism was fundamentally a *socialist* political practice, not merely a style of film focused on re-creating the "real." Jameson writes that "realism is to be conceived as the moment in which a 'restricted' code manages to become elaborated or universal."[7] The restricted code is, in this case, the code of the working class, what Raymond Williams would call their "structure of feeling." Elsewhere the philosopher Gilles Deleuze also recognized that neorealism was crucial, situating it at the conceptual turning point from the relatively reified and dominant "movement-image" to the emancipatory "time-image" in his work *Cinema 1 & 2*.

Here's how Bruno Reichlin recently described neorealism in Italian literature: "A surgical examination of matters of society, an almost documentary attention to the everyday, an adherence in thought and language to the social origins and personalities of the characters, a more-or-less direct criticism of current society and morals."[8] I suggest that game studies should follow these same arguments and not turn to a theory of realism in gaming as mere realistic representation, but define realist games as those games that reflect critically on the minutiae of everyday life, replete as it is with struggle, personal drama, and injustice.

This theoretical project is already beginning in Gonzalo Frasca's work. His essay "Videogames of the Oppressed" examines how games are able to raise social and political issues.[9] As a game designer, Frasca is also interested in the genre he calls "newsgaming," that is, games based on actual news events. His game *September 12th, a Toy World* deals with the war on terrorism, although using the somewhat un-realistic visual idiom of a cartoon-drawn, Web-based bombing game. Other games such as *911 Survivor* and *Waco Resurrection* directly reference current geopolitical events. The game company Kuma refers to this genre as "reality games" and offers its own *Kuma\War* game with episodes ripped directly from firefights in Iraq and Afghanistan.

The Congruence Requirement

The games discussed thus far all strive for a high level of realisticness. But as I have tried to show, social realism is an entirely different matter from mere realistic representation. How can one find true realism in gaming? Is social realism even possible in the medium of the video game, where each pixel is artificially created by the machine? What would it mean for the concept of "play," a word that connotes experimentation and creativity as much as it does infantilizing, apolitical trivialities? (In point of fact, play has started to become politically nontrivial in recent years. "We are living through a movement from an organic, industrial society to a polymorphous, information system," wrote Donna Haraway, "from all work to all play, a deadly game."[10] With the growing significance of immaterial labor, and the concomitant increase in cultivation and exploitation of play—creativity, innovation, the new, the singular, flexibility, the supplement—as a productive force, play will become more and more linked to broad social structures of control. Today we are no doubt witnessing the end of play as politically progressive, or even politically neutral.)

To find social realism in gaming, one must follow the telltale traits of social critique and through them uncover the beginnings of a realist gaming aesthetic. To be sure, there is not a realist game yet like de Sica's *The Bicycle Thief* is to film. But there are games that begin to approximate the core aesthetic values of realism, and I will describe a few of them here. (Protorealism, not realism, might be a better title for these games.)

Forty years of electronic games have come and gone, and only now does one see the emergence of social realism. *State of Emergency*, the riot game from Rockstar Games, has some of these protorealist qualities. The game co-opts the spirit of violent social upheaval seen in events like the Rodney King rebellion in Los Angeles and transposes it into a participatory gaming environment. The game is rife with absurdities and excesses and in no way accurately depicts the brutal realities of urban violence. So in that sense, it fails miserably at realism. But it also retains a realist core. While the game is more or less realistically rendered, its connection to realism is seen primarily in the representation of marginalized communities (disenfranchised

State of Emergency, VIS Entertainment, 2001

youth, hackers, ethnic minorities, and so on), but also in the narrative itself, a fantasy of unbridled, orgiastic anticorporate rebellion.
The game slices easily through the apathy found in much mass media
today, instructing players to "smash the corporation" and giving them
the weapons to do so.

The Swiss art group Etoy also achieved protorealism in gaming
with their online multiplayer game *Toywar*. Part artwork, part game,
and part political intervention, this massively multiplayer online
game was cobbled together in a few quick weeks of programming. The
goal of the game was to fight against the dot-com toy retailer eToys
.com by negatively affecting their stock price on the NASDAQ market. The toy retailer had recently sent a lawsuit to Etoy for trademark
infringement due to the similarity of the two organizations' names.
Many considered the lawsuit bogus. But instead of battling their corporate rivals in court, Etoy went public and turned the whole fiasco
into an online game, enlisting the public to fight the lawsuit on their
behalf.[11] The *Toywar* battlefield, which was online for only a few
months, is a complex, self-contained system, with its own internal
e-mail, its own monetary system, its own social actors, geography, hazards, heroes, and martyrs. Players were able to launch "media bombs"

and other public relations stunts aimed at increasing public dissatisfaction toward eToys.com's lawsuit. In the first two weeks of *Toywar*, eToys.com's stock price on the NASDAQ plummeted by over 50 percent and continued to nose-dive. Of course, eToys.com's stock price was also crashing due to the general decline of the Internet economic bubble, but this economic fact only accentuated the excitement of gameplay. Eventually a few billion dollars of the company's stock value disappeared from the NASDAQ, and the toy retailer declared bankruptcy. Whereas *State of Emergency* prodded gamers to smash a hypothetical corporate thug, *Toywar* gave them a chance to battle a real one. And this is the crucial detail that makes *Toywar* a realist game, for, like a simulation or training game, *Toywar* constructed a meaningful relationship between the affective actions of gamers and the real social contexts in which they live. This is not to say that realism in gaming requires an instrumental cause and effect between the gamer's thumbs on the controller and some consequence in the so-called real world—not at all; that would return us to the trap of the Columbine theory. (The problem of the Columbine theory is, to put it bluntly, one of directionality. Realism in gaming is about the extension of one's own social life. The Columbine theory claims the reverse, that games can somehow exert "realistic" effects back onto the gamer.) Instead I suggest there must be some kind of congruence, some type of *fidelity of context* that transliterates itself from the social reality of the gamer, through one's thumbs, into the game environment and back again. This is what I call the "congruence requirement," and it is necessary for achieving realism in gaming. Without it there is no true realism.

Are Military Games Realist?

With the congruence requirement in mind, it is important to make a distinction between games that are modeled around real events and ones that actually claim to be an extension of real-life struggle (via virtual training sessions or politically utopian fantasies). This brings us to *America's Army*, the military shooter designed and published by the U.S. Army. What is interesting about *America's Army* is not the debate over whether it is thinly veiled propaganda or a legitimate recruitment tool, for it is unabashedly and decisively both, but rather that the central conceit of the game is one of mimetic realism. *America's Army*, quite literally, is about the American army. Because it was developed by the American army and purports to model the experience of the American army, the game can claim a real material referent in ways that other military games—*Delta Force*, *SOCOM*, and so on—simply cannot. So one might think that *America's Army* is a realist game par excellence. But following the definition of realism stated earlier and my "congruence requirement," it is clear that *America's Army* does not achieve realism on either account. As Bruno Reichlin observed, realism requires "a more-or-less direct criticism of current society and morals," which *America's Army* does not do, nor does it aspire to do. In fact, the game can be viewed in exactly the opposite framework: as a bold and brutal reinforcement of current American society and its positive moral perspective on military intervention, be it the war on terrorism or "shock and awe" in Iraq. Further, as Jameson shows us, realism happens in certain moments when "a 'restricted' code" captured from out of the subjugated classes "manages to become elaborated or universal." Again *America's Army* does nothing of the sort. If the U.S. Army has a discursive code, it is certainly not restricted but well articulated and wide reaching. It needs no further assistance in its elaboration. It comes to us already expressed in everything from television recruitment advertisements to multi-billion-dollar procurement bills. And as for the congruence requirement, it fails too if not even a scrap of basic realism is achieved. But even so, one cannot claim there to be a fidelity of context between a civilian American teenager shooting enemies in *America's Army* and the everyday minutiae of that civilian teenager, the specificities of his or her social life in language, culture, and tradition. These war games may be fun, they may be well designed, but they are not realist.

By itself *America's Army* is not that successful as a realist text. However, when put in dialogue with two other games, *America's Army* may be seen in a new light as the realist fantasy or illusion it is. These two games are *Special Force*, released by the Lebanese organization Hizbullah, and *Under Ash*, released by the Syrian publisher Dar Al-Fikr.[12] The ideological opposite of *America's Army*, these two games are

America's Army, U.S. Army, 2002

first-person shooters played from the perspective of a young Palestinian participating in the Islamic jihad. They are, in a sense, the same
militaristic narrative as American-made shooters, but seen instead
from the Islamic fighter's point of view, just as the narrative of *Oppos-
ing Force* reverses the perspective of its predecessor *Half-Life*. (The
obvious militaristic fantasy then, of course, is to network players in
Damascus against players in the Israel Defense Forces and battle this
thing out in virtual space.) These Palestinian first-person shooters
have roughly the look and feel of *America's Army*, albeit without the
virtuoso photorealism of detailed texturing, fog, and deep resolution
available in the army's commercially licensed graphics engine. What
differs is narrative, not representation. If one is to take the definition
of realism given earlier—a documentary-like attention to the everyday struggles of the disenfranchised, leading to a direct criticism of
current social policy—then *Special Force* and *Under Ash* are among
the first truly realist games in existence.

Published by the Central Internet Bureau of Hizbullah, *Special Force*
is a first-person shooter based on the armed Islamic movement in
South Lebanon. The narrative of the game is delivered mostly through
text-based briefings presented at the beginning of each level, which
initiate the player character as a holy warrior fighting against Israeli

America's Army

occupation. The gameplay itself, however, does not carry a strong narrative message, except for sprinklings of pro-intifada and anti-Israeli iconography. The gameplay is based instead on combat scenarios common in first-person shooter games such as traversing minefields, killing enemies, and so on. So while the action in *Special Force* is quite militaristic, it feels like a simple role reversal, a transplant of its American counterparts, with Israelis as the enemies rather than Muslims. The realism of the game is simply its startling premise, that the Palestinian movement is in fact able to depict its own "restricted code" in a shooter game.

Under Ash, from Damascus, depicts a young Palestinian man during the intifada. The game turns the tables on Israeli occupation, letting the gamer fight back, as it were, first with stones, then with guns. The game is not fantasy escapism but instead takes on an almost documentary quality, depicting scenarios from the occupied territories such as the demolishing of Palestinian houses. Combat is central to the narrative, but killing civilians is penalized. In addition, the game is distinctly difficult to play, a sardonic instance of sociopolitical realism in a land fraught with bloodletting on both sides.

Whereas *Special Force* is unapologetically vehement in its depiction of anti-Israeli violence, *Under Ash* takes a more sober, almost

Special Force, Hizbullah Central Internet Bureau, 2003

educational tone. The game's designers describe *Under Ash* as acting in opposition to what they call "American style" power and violence. Realizing that Palestinian youths will most likely want to play shooter games one way or another, the designers of *Under Ash* aim to intervene in the gaming market with a homegrown alternative allowing those youths to play from their own perspective as Palestinians, not as surrogate Americans (as playing SOCOM would surreptitiously force them to do). *Under Ash* players, then, have a personal investment in the struggle depicted in the game, just as they have a personal investment in the struggle happening each day around them. This is something rarely seen in the consumer gaming market. The game does nothing to critique the formal qualities of the genre, however. Instead it is a cookie-cutter repurposing of an American-style shooter for the ideological needs of the Palestinian situation. The engine is the same, but the narrative is different.

Now, contrasted with these Palestinian games, *America's Army* does in fact achieve a sort of sinister realism, for it can't help but foreground its own social ideology. It is not a subjugated ideology, but it is indeed an expression of political realities as they exist today in global military power struggles. Statistics on public opinion illustrate that the average American teenager playing *America's Army* quite possibly *does* harbor a strong nationalistic perspective on world events (even though he or she may be leery of actual war and might never fight in America's real army). The game articulates this perspective. Again, this is not true realism, but like it or not, it is a real articulation of the political advantage felt and desired by the majority of Americans. It takes a game like *Special Force*, with all of Hizbullah's terror in the background, to see the stark, gruesome reality of *America's Army* in the foreground.

The Affect of the Gamer

Now my congruence requirement becomes more clear. It boils down to the affect of the gamer and whether the game is a dreamy, fantastical diversion from that affect, or whether it is a figurative extension of it. With *Special Force* and *Under Ash*—and earlier, but in a more complicated fashion, with *America's Army*—there emerges a true congruence between the real political reality of the gamer and the ability of the game to mimic and extend that political reality, thereby satisfying the unrequited desires contained within it.

As I stress, games are an active medium that requires constant physical input by the player: action, doing, pressing buttons, controlling, and so on. Because of this, a realist game must be realist in doing, in action. And because the primary phenomenological reality of games is that of action (rather than looking, as it is with cinema in what Jameson described as "rapt, mindless fascination"), it follows in a structural sense that the player has a more intimate relationship with the apparatus itself, and therefore with the deployment of realism. The player is significantly more than a mere audience member, but significantly less than a diegetic character. It is the act of doing, of manipulating the controller, that imbricates the player with the game.

So it is because games are an active medium that realism in gaming requires a special congruence between the social reality depicted in the game and the social reality known and lived by the player. This is something never mandated in the history of realist film and may happen only occasionally in gaming depending on the game and the social context of the player. If one is a Hollywood filmmaker, the challenge is simply to come up with a realistic representation of reality. Or if one is a realist filmmaker, the challenge is to capture the social realities, in some capacity, of the disadvantaged classes. But because of the congruence requirement in gaming, if one is a realist game designer, the challenge is not only to capture the social realities of the disenfranchised but also to inject the game back into the correct social milieu of available players where it rings true.

From this one may deduce that realism in gaming is about a relationship between the game and the player. Not a causal relationship, as the Columbine theory might suggest, but a relationship nonetheless. This is one of the primary reasons why video games absolutely cannot be excised from the social contexts in which they are played. To put it bluntly, a typical American youth playing *Special Force* is most likely not experiencing realism, whereas realism is indeed possible for a young Palestinian gamer playing *Special Force* in the occupied territories. This fidelity of context is key for realism in gaming.

Video games reside in a third moment of realism. The first two are realism in narrative (literature) and realism in images (painting, photography, film). For video games, it is realism in action. This brings us back to Aristotle and the *Poetics*, to be sure, but more particularly to Augusto Boal, for whom Aristotle was "coercive," and to Bertolt Brecht. Whereas the visual arts compel viewers to engage in the act of looking, video games, like a whole variety of digital media, compel players to perform acts. Any game that depicts the real world must grapple with this question of action. In this way, realism in gaming is fundamentally a process of revisiting the material substrate of the medium and establishing correspondences with specific activities existent in the social reality of the gamer. Indeed, in the next chapter, I hope to show how all video games may be interpreted in relation to the current information society, what Deleuze called the society of control.

4

Allegories of Control

Playing the Algorithm

With the progressive arrival of new forms of media over the last century or so and perhaps earlier there appears a sort of lag time, call it the "thirty-year rule," starting from the invention of a medium and ending at its ascent to proper and widespread functioning in culture at large. This can be said of film, from its birth at the end of the nineteenth century up to the blossoming of classical film form in the 1930s, or of the Internet with its long period of relatively hidden formation during the 1970s and 1980s only to erupt on the popular stage in the mid-1900s. And we can certainly say the same thing today about video games: what started as a primitive pastime in the 1960s has through the present day experienced its own evolution from a simple to a more sophisticated aesthetic logic, such that one might predict a coming golden age for video games into the next decade not unlike what film experienced in the late 1930s and 1940s.[1] Games like *Final Fantasy X* or *Grand Theft Auto III* signal the beginning of this new golden age. Still, video games reside today in a distinctly lowbrow corner of contemporary society and thus have yet to be held aloft as an art form on par with those of the highest cultural production.

This strikes me as particularly attractive, for one may approach video games today as a type of beautifully undisturbed processing of contemporary life, as yet unmarred by bourgeois exegeses of the format. But how may one critically approach these video games, these uniquely *algorithmic* cultural objects? Certainly they would have something revealing to say about life inside today's global informatic networks. They might even suggest a new approach to critical interpretation itself, one that is as computercentric as its object of study. Philippe Sollers wrote in 1967 that interpretation concerns "The punctuation, the *scanning*, the spatialization of texts"; a year later Roland Barthes put it like this: "the space of writing is to be scanned, not pierced."[2] And a few years later, Jameson adopted a similar vocabulary: "Allegorical interpretation is a type of *scanning* that, *moving back and forth across the text*, readjusts its terms in constant modification of a type quite different from our stereotypes of some static or medieval or biblical decoding."[3] Not coincidentally, these three borrow vocabulary from the realm of electronic machines—the "scanning" of electrons inside a television's screen, or even the scanner/parser modules of a computer compiler—to describe a more contemporary, informatic mode of cultural analysis and interpretation.

Indeed, this same "digitization" of allegorical interpretation, if one may call it that, is evident in film criticism of the 1970s and 1980s, concurrent with the emergence of consumer video machines and the first personal computers. This discourse was inaugurated by the 1970 analysis of John Ford's *Young Mr. Lincoln* written by the editors of *Cahiers du cinéma*. Their reading is aimed at classical Hollywood films, so it has a certain critical relationship to ideology and formal hegemony. Yet they clearly state that their technique is neither an interpretation (getting out something already *in* the film) nor a demystification (digging through manifest meaning to get at latent meaning).

> We refuse to look for "depth," to go from the "literal meaning" to some "secret meaning"; we are not content with what it says (what it intends to say). . . . What will be attempted here through a rescansion of these films in a process of active reading, is to make them say what they have to say *within* what they leave unsaid, to reveal their constituent lacks; these are neither faults in the work . . . nor a deception on the part of the author. . . . They are *structuring absences*.[4]

The influence of computers and informatic networks, of what Gene Youngblood in the same year called the "intermedia network," on the *Cahiers* mentality is unmistakable. Their approach is not a commentary on the inner workings of the cinematic text—as an earlier mode of allegorical interpretation would have required—but a rereading, a rescanning, and ultimately a *word processing* of the film itself. The *Cahiers* style of analysis is what one might term a "horizontal" allegory. It scans the surfaces of texts looking for new interpretive patterns. These patterns are, in essence, allegorical, but they no longer observe the division between what Jameson called the negative hermeneutic of ideology critique on the one hand and the positive hermeneutic of utopian collectivism on the other.[5] This is the crucial point: scanning is wholly different from demystifying. And as two different techniques for interpretation, they are indicative of two very different political and social realities: computerized versus noncomputerized.

Some of Deleuze's later writings are helpful in understanding the division between these two realities. In his "Postscript on Control Societies," a short work from 1990, Deleuze defines two historical periods: first, the "disciplinary societies" of modernity, growing out of the rule of the sovereign, into the "vast spaces of enclosure," the social castings and bodily molds that Michel Foucault has described so well; and second, what Deleuze terms the "societies of control" that inhabit the late twentieth century—these are based around what he calls logics of "modulation" and the "ultrarapid forms of free-floating control."[6] While the disciplinary societies of high modernity were characterized by more physical semiotic constructs such as the signature and the document, today's societies of control are characterized by immaterial ones such as the password and the computer. These control societies are characterized by the networks of genetic science and computers, but also by much more conventional network forms. In each case, though, Deleuze points out how the principle of organization in computer networks has shifted away from confinement and enclosure toward a seemingly infinite extension of controlled mobility:

> A control is not a discipline. In making freeways, for example, you don't enclose people but instead multiply the means of control. I am not saying that this is the freeway's exclusive purpose, but that people

can drive infinitely and "freely" without being at all confined yet
while still being perfectly controlled. This is our future.[7]

Whether it is an information superhighway or a plain old freeway,
what Deleuze defines as control is key to understanding how computerized information societies function. It is part of a larger shift in social
life, characterized by a movement away from central bureaucracies and
vertical hierarchies toward a broad network of autonomous social
actors. As the architect Branden Hookway writes:

> The shift is occurring across the spectrum of information technolo-
> gies as we move from models of the global application of intelligence,
> with their universality and frictionless dispersal, to one of local
> applications, where intelligence is site-specific and fluid.[8]

This shift toward a control society has also been documented in such
varied texts as those of sociologist Manuel Castells, Hakim Bey, and
the Italian autonomist political movement of the 1970s. Even harsh
critics of this shift, such as Nick Dyer-Witheford (author of *Cyber-
Marx*), surely admit that the shift is taking place. It is part of a larger
process of postmodernization that is happening the world over.

What are the symptoms of this social transformation? They are
seen whenever a company like Microsoft outsources a call center from
Redmond to Bangalore, or in the new medical surveillance networks
scanning global health databases for the next outbreak of SARS.
Even today's military has redefined itself around network- and computercentric modes of operation: pilot interfaces for remotely oper-
ated Predator aircraft mimic computer game interfaces; captains in the
U.S. Army learn wartime tactics through video games like *Full Spectrum Command*, a training tool jointly developed by the American
and Singaporean militaries; in the military's Future Combat Systems
initiative, computer networks themselves are classified as weapons
systems.

But these symptoms are mere indices for deeper social maladies,
many of which fall outside the realm of the machine altogether—
even if they are ultimately exacerbated by it. For while Bangalore may
be booming, it is an island of exception inside a country still strug-
gling with the challenges of postcolonialism and unequal moderniza-
tion. Computers have a knack for accentuating social injustice, for

widening the gap between the rich and the poor (as the economists have well documented). Thus the claims I make here about the relationship between video games and the contemporary political situation refer specifically to the social imaginary of the wired world and how the various structures of organization and regulation within it are repurposed into the formal grammar of the medium.

As Jameson illustrates in *Signatures of the Visible*, the translation of political realities into film has a somewhat complicated track record, for mainstream cinema generally deals with the problem of politics not in fact by solving it but by sublimating it. Fifty years ago, Hitchcock showed the plodding, unfeeling machinations of the criminal justice system in his film *The Wrong Man*. Today the police are not removed from the crime film genre, far from it, but their micromovements of bureaucratic command and control are gone. The political sleight of hand of mainstream cinema is that the audience is rarely shown the boring minutiae of discipline and confinement that constitute the various apparatuses of control in contemporary societies. This is precisely why Jameson's interpretive method is so successful. Another example: in John Woo's *The Killer*, not only is the killer above the law (or, more precisely, outside it), but so is the cop, both literally in his final bloody act of extrajudicial vengeance and also figuratively in that one never sees the cuffings, the bookings, the indictments, the court appearances, and all the other details of modern criminality and confinement depicted in *The Wrong Man*. Films like *Bad Boys 2* or *Heat* do the same thing. In fact, most cop flicks eschew this type of representation, rising above the profession, as it were, to convey other things (justice, friendship, honor, or what have you). In other words, discipline and confinement, as a modern control apparatus, are rarely represented today, except when, in singular instances like the Rodney King tape, they erupt onto the screen in gory detail (having first erupted from the bounds of film itself and penetrated the altogether different medium of video). Instead, discipline and confinement are upstaged by other matters, sublimated into other representational forms. The accurate representation of political control is thus eclipsed in much of the cinema (requiring, Jameson teaches us, allegorical interpretation to bring it back to the fore), which is unfortunate, because despite its unsexy screen presence, informatic

Civilization III, Firaxis Games, 2001

control is precisely the most important thing to show on the screen if one wishes to allegorize political power today.

Now, what is so interesting about video games is that they essentially invert film's political conundrum, leading to almost exactly the opposite scenario. Video games don't attempt to hide informatic control; they flaunt it. Look to the auteur work of game designers like Hideo Kojima, Yu Suzuki, or Sid Meier. In the work of Meier, the gamer is not simply playing this or that historical simulation. The gamer is instead learning, internalizing, and becoming intimate with a massive, multipart, global algorithm. To play the game means to play

the code of the game. To win means to know the system. And thus to *interpret* a game means to interpret its algorithm (to discover its parallel "allegorithm").

So today there is a twin transformation: from the modern cinema to the contemporary video game, but also from traditional allegory to what I am calling horizontal or "control" allegory. I suggest that video games are, at their structural core, in direct synchronization with the political realities of the informatic age. If Meier's work is about anything, it is about information society itself. It is about knowing systems and knowing code, or, I should say, knowing *the* system and knowing *the* code. "The way computer games teach structures of thought," writes Ted Friedman on Meier's game series *Civilization*, "is by getting you to internalize the logic of the program. To win, you can't just do whatever you want. You have to figure out what will work within the rules of the game. You must learn to predict the consequences of each move, and anticipate the computer's response. Eventually, your decisions become intuitive, as smooth and rapid-fire as the computer's own machinations."[9] Meier makes no effort to hide this essential characteristic behind a veil, either, as would popular cinema. The massive electronic network of command and control that I have elsewhere called "protocol" is precisely the visible, active, essential, and core ingredient of Meier's work in particular and video games in general. You can't miss it. Lev Manovich agrees with Friedman: "[Games] demand that a player can execute an algorithm in order to win. As the player proceeds through the game, she gradually discovers the rules that operate in the universe constructed by this game. She learns its hidden logic—in short, its algorithm."[10] So while games have linear narratives that may appear in broad arcs from beginning to end, or may appear in cinematic segues and interludes, they also have nonlinear narratives that must unfold in algorithmic form during gameplay. In this sense, video games deliver to the player the power relationships of informatic media firsthand, choreographed into a multivalent cluster of play activities. In fact, in their very core, video games do nothing but present contemporary political realities in relatively unmediated form. They solve the problem of political control, not by sublimating it as does the cinema, but by *making it coterminous with the entire game*, and in this way video games achieve a unique type of political transparency.

Buckminster Fuller articulated the systemic, geopolitical characteristics of gaming decades before in his "World Game" and World Design Initiative of the 1960s. The World Game was to be played on a massive "stretched out football field sized world map." The game map was "wired throughout so that mini-bulbs, installed all over its surface, could be lighted by the computer at appropriate points to show various, accurately positioned, proportional data regarding world conditions, events, and resources." Fuller's game was a global resource management simulation, not unlike Meier's *Civilization*. But the object of Fuller's game was "to explore for ways to make it possible for

"City View," *Civilization III*

anybody and everybody in the human family to enjoy the total earth without any human interfering with any other human and without any human gaining advantage at the expense of another." While Fuller's game follows the same logic of *Civilization* or other global algo-rithm games, his political goals were decidedly more progressive, as he showed in a jab at the American mathematician John von Neu-mann: "In playing the game I propose that we set up a different sys-tem of games from that of Dr. John Von Neumann whose 'Theory of Games' was always predicated upon one side losing 100 percent. His game theory is called 'Drop Dead.' In our World Game we propose to explore and test by assimilated adoption various schemes of 'How to Make the World Work.' To win the World Game everybody must be made physically successful. Everybody must win."[11]

So, broadly speaking, there is an extramedium shift in which films about the absence of control have been replaced by games that fetishize control. But there is simultaneously an intermedium shift, happening predominantly within the cinema. What Jameson called the conspiracy film of the 1970s (*All the President's Men*, *The Parallax View*) became no longer emblematic at the start of the new millennium. Instead, films of epistemological reversal have become prominent, mutating out of the old whodunit genre. David Fincher is the contemporary counterpart to Alan Pakula in this regard, with *The Game* and *Fight Club* as masterpieces of epistemological reversal, but one need only point to the preponderance of other films grounded in mind-bending trickery of reality and illusion (*Jagged Edge*, *The Usual Suspects*, *The Matrix*, *The Cell*, *eXistenZ*, *The Sixth Sense*, *Wild Things*, and so on, or even with games like Hideo Kojima's *Metal Gear* series) to see how the cinema has been delivered from the oppression of unlocatable capitalism (as in Jameson's view) only to be sentenced to a new oppression of disingenuous informatics. For every moment that the conspiracy film rehashes the traumas of capitalism in the other-form of monumental modern architecture, as with the Space Needle at the start of *The Parallax View*, the knowledge-reversal film aims at doling out data to the audience, but only to show at the last minute how everything was otherwise. The digital can't exert control with architecture, so it does it with information. The genre offers a type of epistemological challenge to the audience: follow a roller coaster of reversals and revelations, and the viewer will eventually achieve informatic truth in the end. I see this fetishization of the "knowledge triumph" as a sort of informatization of the conspiracy film described by Jameson.

But back to video games and how exactly the operator "plays the algorithm." This happens most vividly in many console games, in which intricate combinations of buttons must be executed with precise timing to accomplish something in the game. Indeed, games like

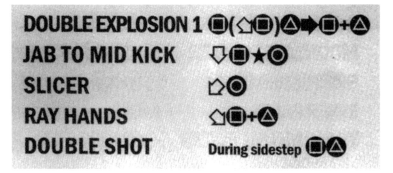

Tekken Tag Tournament, Namco, 1994

Tekken or *Tony Hawk's Pro Skater* hinge on the operator's ability to motor-memorize button combinations for specific moves. The algorithms for such moves are usually documented in the game sleeve by using a coded notation similar to tablature for music ("Up + X-X-O" on a PlayStation controller, for example). Newcomers to such games are often derided as mere "button mashers." But in a broader sense, let us return to Sid Meier and see what it means to play the algorithm at the macro level.

Ideological Critique

After the initial experience of playing *Civilization* there are perhaps three successive phases that one passes through on the road to critiquing this particularly loaded cultural artifact. The first phase is often an immense chasm of pessimism arising from the fear that *Civilization* in particular and video games in general are somehow immune to meaningful interpretation, that they are somehow outside criticism. Yes, games are about algorithms, but what exactly does that matter when it comes to cultural critique? Perhaps video games *have* no politics? This was, most likely, the same sensation faced by others attempting to critique hitherto mystified artifacts of popular culture — Janice Radway with the romance novel, Dick Hebdige with punk style, or Roland Barthes with the striptease. Often it is precisely those places in culture that appear politically innocent that are at the end of the day the most politically charged. Step two, then, consists of the slow process of ideological critique using the telltale clues contained in the game to connect it with larger social processes. (Here is where Caillois, presented in chapter 1 as essentially apolitical, returns with a penetrative observation about the inherent political potential of games, vis-à-vis the question of demystification and institutional critique. Reacting to Huizinga, Caillois writes that "without doubt, secrecy, mystery, and even travesty can be transformed into play activity, but it must be immediately pointed out that this transformation is necessarily to the detriment of the secret and mysterious, which play exposes, publishes, and somehow *expends*. In a word, play tends to remove the very nature of the mysterious. On the other hand, when the secret, the mask, or the costume fulfills a sacramental function one can be sure that not play, but an institution is involved.")[12] Critiquing the ideological content of video games is what Katie Salen and Eric Zimmerman, following Brian Sutton-Smith on play, refer to as the "cultural rhetoric" of games.[13] For *Civilization*, the political histories of state and national powers coupled with the rise of the information society seem particularly apropos. One might then construct a vast ideological critique of the game, focusing on its explicit logocentrism, its nationalism and imperialism, its expansionist logic, as well as its implicit racism and classism.

Just as medieval scholars used the existence of contradiction in a text as indication of the existence of allegory, so *Civilization* has within it many contradictions that suggest such an allegorical interpretation. One example is the explicit mixing of ahistorical logic, such as the founding of a market economy in a place called "London" in 4000 BC, with the historical logic of scientific knowledge accumulation or cultural development. Another is the strange mixing of isometric perspective for the foreground and traditional perspective for the background in the "City View."

The expansionist logic of the game is signified both visually and spatially. "At the beginning of the game," Friedman writes, "almost all of the map is black; you don't get to learn what's out there until one of your units has explored the area. Gradually, as you expand your empire and send out scouting parties, the landscape is revealed."[14] These specific conventions within both the narrative and the visual signification of the game therefore reward expansionism, even require it. Meier's *Alpha Centauri* mimics these semiotic conventions but ups the ante by positioning the player in the ultimate expansionist haven, outer space. This has the added bonus of eliminating concerns about the politics of expansionist narratives, for, one assumes, it is easier to rationalize killing anonymous alien life-forms in *Alpha Centauri* than it is killing Zulus in *Civilization III*. Expansionism has, historically, always had close links with racism; the expansionism of the colonial period of modernity, for example, was rooted in a specific philosophy about the superiority of European culture, religion, and so on, over that of the Asiatic, African, and American native peoples. Again we turn to Meier, who further developed his expansionist vision in 1994 with *Colonization*, a politically dubious game modeled on the software

Colonization, Micro Prose, 1995

engine used in *Civilization* and set in the period between the discovery of the New World and the American Revolution. The American Indians in this game follow a less-than-flattering historical stereotype, both in their onscreen depiction and in terms of the characteristics and abilities they are granted as part of the algorithm. Later, in *Civilization III*, Meier expanded his stereotyping to include sixteen historical identities, from the Aztecs and the Babylonians to the French and the Russians. In this game, one learns that the Aztecs are "religious" but not "industrious," characteristics that affect their various proclivities in the gamic algorithm, while the Romans are "militaristic" but, most curiously, not "expansionist." Of course, this sort of typing is but a few keystrokes away from a world in which blacks are "athletic" and women are "emotional." That the game tactfully avoids these more blatant offenses does not exempt it from endorsing a logic that prizes the classification of humans into types and the normative labeling of those types.

Worse than attributing a specific characteristic to a specific racial or national group is the fact that ideological models such as these ignore the complexity, variation, and rich diversity of human life at many

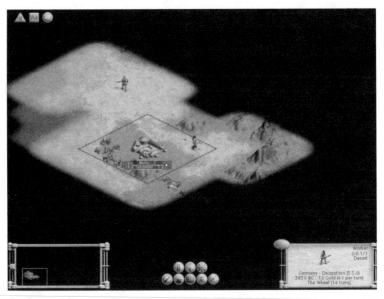

Civilization III

levels: the *Civilization III* algorithm ignores change over time (Tsarist Russia versus Soviet Russia); it erases any number of other peoples existing throughout history the Inuit, the Irish, and on and on; it conflates a civilization with a specific national or tribal identity and ignores questions of hybridity and diaspora such as those of African Americans or Jews. In short, it transposes the many-layered quality of social life to an inflexible, reductive algorithm for "civilization"—a process not dissimilar to what Marxists call reification, only updated for the digital age. (The reason for doing this is, of course, a practical one: to create balanced gameplay, game designers require an array of variables that can be tweaked and tuned across the various environments and characters.) And while one needs no further proof of the game's dubious political assumptions, I might point out that the game is also a folly of logocentrism; it is structured around a quest for knowledge, with all human thought broken down into neatly packaged discoveries that are arranged in a branching time line where one discovery is a precondition for the next. But so much for ideological scrutiny.

Civilization	Commercial	Expansionist	Industrious	Militaristic	Religious	Scientific
Americans		X	X			
Aztecs				X	X	
Babylonians					X	X
Chinese			X	X		
Egyptians			X		X	
English	X	X				
French	X		X			
Germans	X	X				
Greeks	X					X
Indians	X				X	
Iroquois		X			X	
Japanese				X	X	
Persians			X			X
Romans	X			X		
Russians		X				X
Zulus		X		X		

"Civilization Characteristics," *Civilization III*

Informatic Critique

In conjunction with these manifest political investigations, the third step is to elaborate a formal critique rooted in the core principles of informatics that serve as the foundation of the gaming format. The principles adopted by Manovich in *The Language of New Media* might be a good place to begin: numerical representation, modularity, automation, variability, and transcoding. But to state this would simply be to state the obvious, that *Civilization* is new media. The claim that *Civilization* is a control allegory is to say something different: that the game plays the very codes of informatic control today. So what are the core principles of informatic control? Beyond Manovich, I would supplement the discussion with an analysis of what are called the protocols of digital technology. The Internet protocols, for example, consist of approximately three thousand technical documents published to date outlining the necessary design specifications for specific technologies like the Internet Protocol (IP) or Hypertext Markup Language (HTML). These documents are called RFCs (Request for Comments). The expression "request for comments" derives from a memorandum titled "Host Software" sent by Steve Crocker on April 7, 1969 (which is known today as RFC number 1) and is indicative of the collaborative, open nature of protocol authorship (one is reminded of Deleuze's "freeways"). Called "the primary documentation of the Internet,"[15] these technical memorandums detail the vast majority of standards and protocols used today on game consoles like the Xbox as well as other types of networked computers.[16]

Flexibility is one of the core political principles of informatic control, described both by Deleuze in his theorization of "control society" and by computer scientists like Crocker. The principle derives from the scientist Paul Baran's pioneering work on distributed networks, which prizes flexibility as a strategy for avoiding technical failure at the system level. Flexibility is still one of the core principles of Internet protocol design, perhaps best illustrated by the routing functionality of IP, which is able to move information through networks in an ad hoc, adaptable manner. The concept of flexibility is also central to the new information economies, powering innovations in fulfillment, customization, and other aspects of what is known as "flexible accumulation." While it might appear liberating or utopian, don't be fooled; flexibility is one of the founding principles of global informatic control. It is to the control society what discipline was to a previous one.

Flexibility is allegorically repurposed in *Civilization* via the use of various sliders and parameters to regulate flow and create systemic equilibrium. All elements in the game are put in quantitative, dynamic relationships with each other, such that a "Cultural Victory" conclusion of the game is differentiated from a "Conquest Victory" conclusion only through slight differences in the two algorithms for winning. The game is able to adjust and compensate for whatever outcome the operator pursues. Various coefficients and formulas (the delightfully named "Governor governor," for example) are tweaked to achieve balance in gameplay.

What flexibility allows for is universal standardization (another crucial principle of informatic control). If diverse technical systems

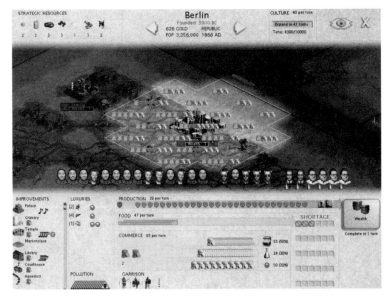

Civilization III

are *flexible* enough to accommodate massive contingency, then the result is a more robust system that can subsume all comers under the larger mantle of continuity and universalism. The Internet protocol white papers say it all: "Be conservative in what you do, be liberal in what you accept from others."[17] The goal of total subsumption goes hand in hand with informatic control. The massive "making equivalent" in *Civilization*—the making equivalent of different government types (the most delicious detail in early versions of Meier's game is the pull-down menu option for starting a revolution), of different victory options, of formulaically equating n number of happy citizens with the availability of luxuries, and so on—is, in this sense, an allegorical reprocessing of the universal standardizations that go into the creation of informatic networks today. In Meier, game studies looks more like game theory.

In contrast to my previous ideological concerns, the point now is not whether the *Civilization* algorithm embodies a specific ideology of "soft" racism, or even whether it embodies the core principles of new media adopted from Manovich, but whether it embodies the logic of informatic control itself. Other simulations let the gamer play the logic of a plane (*Flight Simulator*, or Meier's own flying games from the 1980s), the logic of a car (*Gran Turismo*), or what have you. But with *Civilization*, Meier has simulated the total logic of informatics itself.

But now we are at an impasse, for the more one allegorizes informatic control in *Civilization*, the more my previous comments about ideology start to unravel. And the more one tries to pin down the ideological critique, the more one sees that such a critique is undermined by the existence of something altogether different from ideology: informatic code. So where the ideological critique succeeds, it fails. Instead of offering better clues, the ideological critique (traditional allegory) is undermined by its own revelation of the protocological critique (control allegory). In video games, at least, one trumps the other. Consider my previous claims about Meier's construction of racial and national identity: the more one examines the actual construction of racial and national identity in the game, the more one sees that identity itself is an entirely codified affair within the logic of the software. Identity is a data type, a mathematical variable. The construction of identity in *Civilization* gains momentum from offline racial typing, to be sure, but then moves further to a specifically informatic mode of cybernetic typing: capture, transcoding, statistical analysis, quantitative profiling (behavioral or biological), keying attributes to specific numeric variables, and so on. This is similar to what Manovich calls the logic of selection—or what Lisa Nakamura calls "menu-driven identities"—only now Manovich's pick-and-choose, window-shopper logic of graphical interfaces governs a rather distinct set of human identity attributes. As Nakamura laments, "Who can—or wants to—claim a perfectly pure, legible identity that can be fully expressed by a decision tree designed by a corporation?"[18] So the skin tone parameters for player character construction in everything from *Sissyfight* to *World of Warcraft* are not an index for older, offline constructions of race and identity, although they are a direct extension of this larger social history, but instead an index for the very dominance of informatic organization and how it has entirely overhauled, revolutionized, and recolonized the function of identity. In *Civilization*, identity is modular, instrumental, typed, numerical, algorithmic. To use history as another example: the more one begins to think that *Civilization* is about a certain ideological interpretation of history (neoconservative, reactionary, or what have you), or even that it creates a computer-generated "history effect," the more one realizes that it is about the absence of history altogether, or rather, the transcoding of history into specific mathematical models. History is what hurts, wrote Jameson—history is the slow, negotiated struggle of individuals together with others in their material reality. The modeling of history in computer code, even using Meier's sophisticated algorithms, can only ever be a reductive exercise of capture and transcoding. So "history" in *Civilization* is precisely the opposite of history, not because the game fetishizes the imperial perspective, but because the diachronic details of lived life are replaced by the synchronic homogeneity of code pure and simple. It is a new sort of fetish altogether. (To be entirely clear: mine is an argument about informatic control, not about ideology; a politically progressive "*People's Civilization*" game, à la Howard Zinn, would beg the same critique.) Thus the logic of informatics and horizontality is privileged over the logic of ideology and verticality in this game, as it mostly likely is in all video games in varying degrees.

So this is not unique to *Civilization*. The other great simulation game that has risen above the limitations of the genre is *The Sims*, but instead of seizing on the totality of informatic control as a theme, this game does the reverse, diving down into the banality of technology, the muted horrors of a life lived as an algorithm. As I have alluded to in Jameson, the depth model in traditional allegorical interpretation is a sublimation of the separation felt by the viewer between his or her experience of consuming the media and the potentially liberating political value of that media. But video games abandon this dissatisfying model of deferral, epitomizing instead the flatness of control allegory by unifying the act of playing the game with an immediate political experience. In other words, *The Sims* is a game that delivers its own political critique up front as part of the gameplay. There is no need for the critic to unpack the game later. The boredom, the sterility, the uselessness, and the futility of contemporary life appear precisely through those things that represent them best: a middleclass suburban house, an Ikea catalog of personal possessions, crappy food and even less appetizing music, the same dozen mindless tasks over and over—how can one craft a better critique of contemporary life? This is the politically dubious, but nonetheless revealing, quality of play identified by Adorno in the supplement to his *Aesthetic Theory*: "Playful forms are without exception forms of repetition"; "In art, play is from the outset disciplinary."[19]

As an entire genre, the first-person shooter also illustrates this type of allegorical interpretation of info-politics. Dash the naysayers, the shooter is an allegory of liberation pure and simple. This complicated genre is uncomplicated. There can be no better format for encoding and reprocessing the unvarnished exertion of affective force. I think of *Unreal Tournament* or *Counter-Strike* as the final realization of André Breton's dream of the purest surrealist act: the desire to burst into the street with a pistol, firing quickly and blindly at anyone complicit with what he called "the petty system of debasement and cretinization." The shooter as genre and the shooter as act are bound together in an intimate unity. The shooter is not a stand-in for activity. It *is* activity. (Just as the game is not a stand-in for informatics but *is* informatics.) The experience of the shooter is a "smooth" experience, to use Deleuze and Guattari's term, whereby its various components have yet to be stratified and differentiated, as text on one side and reading or looking on the other. In this sense, the aesthetics of gaming often lack any sort of deep representation (to the extent that representation requires both meaning and the encoding of meaning in material form). Allegory has collapsed back to a singularity in gaming. In fact, the redundancy in the vocabulary says it all: "the cultural logic of informatics." The activity of gaming, which, as I've stressed over and over, only ever comes into being when the game is actually played, is an *undivided* act wherein meaning and doing transpire in the same gamic gesture.

A Theory of Pretending

This last point may be recontextualized through a fundamental observation about video games made at the outset of this book, that games let one *act*. In fact, they require it; video games are actions. Now, following the definition of literary allegory as "other-speak,"[20] I must define the gamic allegory: it is "other-act." The interpretation of gamic acts, then, should be thought of as the creation of a secondary discourse narrating a series of "other-acts." A century ago, Maurice Blondel suggested the word "allergy," following his theory of "coaction" or "another's action."[21] Blondel's use of the term assumes the existence of more than one individual, yet it is still an interesting influence because of his focus on parallel actions. Coaction proper in the context of video gaming would mean something like multiplayer action, which itself would need to be supplemented with a reading of the allegorical multiact. Either way, the interpretation of gamic acts is the process of understanding what it means to *do* something and mean something else. It is a science of the "as if." The customary definition of allegory as "extended metaphor" should, for games, be changed to "*enacted* metaphor." (In fact, for their active duality, zeugma or syllepsis are even more evocative figures of speech.) When one plays *Civilization,* there is one action taking place, but there is more than one significant action taking place. This is the parallelism necessitated by allegory. The first half of the parallelism is the actual playing of the game, but the other is the playing of informatics. For video games, one needs a *theory of pretending,* but only in the most positive sense of the term, as a theory of actions that have multiple meanings.

Again, Bateson: "The playful nip denotes the bite, but it does not denote what would be denoted by the bite."[22] So the roll of control allegory is—methodologically but not structurally—to see the nip and process neither the nip nor the bite, but instead what the bite denotes. I say methodologically but not structurally because there is no camouflage here: the playful video game may metacommunicate "this is play," but it can never avoid also being informatic control.

In this sense, I suggest that the game critic should be concerned not only with the interpretation of linguistic signs, as in literary studies or film theory, but also with the interpretation of *polyvalent doing.* This has always been an exciting terrain for hermeneutics, albeit less well traveled, and in it one must interpret material action instead of keeping to the relatively safe haven of textual analysis.

The critical terrain has likewise shrunk in the age of interactive media from a two-way relationship involving the text and the reader-as-critic to a singular moment involving the gamer (the doer) in the act of gameplay. The game-as-text is now wholly subsumed within the category of the gamer, for he or she creates the gamic text by doing.

This explains the tendency toward control allegory in informatic culture. The primary authors are missing from this formula not because I wish to debase the growing auteur status of game designers, nothing of the sort, but simply because they are no longer directly involved in the moment of interpretation—but this has been the case in interpretive studies for many decades now.

Here, then, are the two allegorical modes compared side by side. Traditional or "deep" allegory seems to have its center of gravity in the early to mid-twentieth century and particularly in the cinematic form (à la Jameson), while control allegory finds its proper consummation in new media in general and video games in particular.

	Deep allegory	Control allegory
Emblematic medium	Cinema	Video games
Political expression	Class struggle	Informatic control
Hermeneutic	Reading	Processing
Parallelism	Other-speak	Other-act

Video games are allegories for our contemporary life under the protocological network of continuous informatic control. In fact, the more emancipating games seem to be as a medium, substituting activity for passivity or a branching narrative for a linear one, the more they are in fact hiding the fundamental social transformation into informatics that has affected the globe during recent decades. In modernity, ideology was an instrument of power, but in postmodernity ideology is a decoy, as I hope to have shown with the game *Civilization*. So a game's revealing is also a rewriting (a lateral step, not a forward one). A game's celebration of the end of ideological manipulation is also a new manipulation, only this time using wholly different diagrams of command and control.

In sum, with the appearance of informatic reprocessing as text—in the style of Sid Meier, but also in everything from turntablism to net.art—allegory no longer consists of a text and another text, but of an enacted text and another enacted text, such that we must now say: to do allegory means to playact, not, as Frye wrote, to allegorize means to write commentary. And hence Deleuze: "The philosopher creates. He doesn't reflect."

5

Countergaming

Artist-Made Game Mods

Artist-made video game mods are an unusual thing, for they seem to contradict their very existence: when the mod rises to the level of art, rather than a gesture of fandom—as *Counter-Strike* was to *Half-Life*—then, more often than not, the game loses its rule set completely and ceases to be a game after all.[1] Jodi's *untitled game* follows this contradictory logic when it ignores all possibility of gameplay in *Quake* and propels the game into fits of abstract modernism. Brody Condon's *Adam Killer* does something similar, transforming what was once fluid gameplay into the brute art of red blood on white clothes and shotgun shells soaring in the air. So if gameplay is part of the core definition of a video game, how can one start to think about mods that usurp gameplay or eliminate it entirely?

What is a video game "mod"? It is a video game that has been modified or otherwise hacked by a user or group of users. A video game may be modified in three basic ways: (1) at the level of its visual design, substituting new level maps, new artwork, new character models, and so on; (2) at the level of the rules of the game, changing how gameplay unfolds—who wins, who loses, and what the repercussions of various gamic acts are; or (3) at the level of its software technology, changing character behavior, game physics, lighting techniques, and so on. But as I suggest, artist mods tend to consider video games as nothing more than game *technologies*, and thus most artist-made video game mods to date are mods of game technologies (whether at the visual level or the physics level), not mods of actual gameplay. Katie Salen describes the situation quite clearly:

> Many artist mods, like Jodi's, are more mods of game engine technology than they are of the games themselves. The interest is not in modifying game play, but in modifying the representational space. Spaces once designed for player interaction, in fact spaces that only gained meaning through interaction, are transformed into spaces to be seen and watched, rather than played.[2]

In other words, contemporary artist-made game mods tend to approach either the visual design of the game (option 1) or the underlying game engine (option 3). Mods of actual gameplay (option 2) are less common, and in fact gameplay is often neglected to the point of disappearance in most artist game mods.

Some mods like *Adam Killer* change only a few key aspects of the game, presenting an unusual scenario and a single visual trick, while others like *r/c* by retroYou (Joan Leandre) contradict the source game almost entirely, changing the core interactivity of the game as well as its visual aesthetic. (When a game is modified in such a wholesale fashion, it is often called a game "conversion" or a "total conversion.") Tilman Baumgärtel writes: "The possibility of making modifications to computer games ('mods' for short) has inspired [media artists] to create their own versions of games that, in some cases, take the premises of the games further and think them through to their logical conclusion and, in others, explicitly contradict them."[3] Indeed, artist-made game mods tend to conflict violently with the mainstream gaming industry's expectations for how games should be designed. They often defy the industry's design style point-for-point, with the goal of disrupting the intuitive flow of gameplay.

Several years ago, Peter Wollen said a similar thing about Jean-Luc Godard and the countercinema of the 1960s. "There are a number of reasons why Godard has broken with narrative transitivity," Wollen

Brody Condon, *Adam Killer*, 1999–2001. Reproduced with permission.

wrote. "Perhaps the most important is that he can disrupt the emotional spell of the narrative and thus force the spectator, by interrupting the narrative flow, to reconcentrate and refocus his attention."[4] The same type of disruption appears in artist-made game mods. For this reason, some have suggested that today there exists a new avantgarde, a "countergaming" movement gravitating around the work of Jodi, Anne-Marie Schleiner, Brody Condon, retroYou, Cory Arcangel, Tom Betts, and others. This movement exists in opposition to and outside the gaming mainstream, and it is this movement that I would like to examine here.

Let me start, then, with Peter Wollen's seven theses on counter-cinema, for they should offer some direction for thinking about the formal grammar of oppositional cultural production. Here he opposes each of the seven "values of the old cinema" (the left-hand term) with those from Godard (the right-hand term):

1. *Narrative Transitivity v. Narrative Intransitivity.* (One thing following another v. gaps and interruptions, episodic construction, undigested digression.)

RetroYou, *R/C 100*, 2001. RetroYou R/C series 1999–2002.

2. *Identification v. Estrangement.* (Empathy, emotional involvement with a character v. direct address, multiple and divided characters, commentary.)

3. *Transparency v. Foregrounding.* ("Language wants to be overlooked"—Siertsema v. making the mechanics of the film/text visible and explicit.)

4. *Single Diegesis v. Multiple Diegesis.* (A unitary homogeneous world v. heterogeneous worlds. Rupture between different codes and different channels.)

5. *Closure v. Aperture.* (A self-contained object, harmonized within its own bounds v. open-endedness, overspill, inter-textuality—allusion, quotation, and parody.)

6. *Pleasure v. Unpleasure.* (Entertainment, aiming to satisfy the spectator v. provocation, aiming to dissatisfy and hence change the spectator.)

7. *Fiction v. Reality.* (Actors wearing makeup, acting a story v. real life, the breakdown of representation, truth.)[5]

These seven points map out a division between classical Hollywood film form and the more experimental techniques practiced in art film. So, for example, to apply Wollen's theoretical framework, when Godard sends his couple out to the country in *Weekend* only for them to be stymied by an excruciatingly long traffic jam (mirrored formally via an excruciatingly long camera shot), he is experimenting with "unpleasure" and "narrative intransitivity." Or when the Italian director Luchino Visconti casts nonprofessional actors for his fishermen in *La terra trema*, he is grappling directly with "reality" and the breakdown of representation, not simply with the "fiction" realism of a Hollywood film like *Sullivan's Travels*, though both depict the hardship of the poor at some level. Or today, in independent films like *Run Lola Run* or *Timecode*, when directors mix and overlay difference spaces and different times, they are engaging the countercinema technique of "multiple diegesis," something rarely seen in the more mainstream narrative cinema. What is so fascinating about countercinema is not simply the identification of alternate formal strategies but the active employment and gleeful exploration of those strategies. Classical film form certainly borrows from the countercinema here and there. So it is a question of commitment to certain techniques, not simply dipping into them from time to time. This parallel universe of formal experimentation, at once divorced from, and supplementary to, mainstream cinema, is what Wollen finds so fascinating in the work of Godard, and it is an arrangement that also exists today in video games.

I said in the beginning that artist-made video game mods undercut themselves to such a degree that they almost cease being games. Of course, this is not altogether true, for important links remain between countergaming and the gaming industry, between mods and their sources. While the countercinema movement described by Wollen existed largely outside Hollywood's commercial machine, game mods are actually promoted by the commercial sector. This is what Brody Condon calls "industry-sanctioned hacking." Since hacking is generally unloved in other sectors (the music industry, the film industry), the fact that the gaming industry allows such activities is quite significant. Anne-Marie Schleiner describes how, at least for PC gaming, the industry has long promoted hacking, patching, and modding by their own consumers:

> In 1994 ID software released the source code for Doom, a 3-d tunnel networkable shooter game, (one year after their release of the game commercially.) Avid players of Doom got their hand on this source code and created editors for making custom Doom levels or what were

Alphaville, directed by Jean-Luc Godard, 1965

referred to as "wads." In 1996 Bungie software bundled the Marathon
series games with Forge and Anvil, game editing software for map
making and inserting new textures, character (sprite) animations,
sounds and physic properties.[6]

Today games continue to be released with level editors and other
mod tools included. Modifying games is almost as natural as playing
them. Indeed, video games lend themselves to the practice of modding
in ways not seen in other media like film or literature. This is primarily due to the technical distinction between the core game engine
and the specific game design and narrative contained within it. A
single game engine may facilitate a wide variety of individual games.
The game engine is a type of abstract core technology that, while it
may exert its own personality through telltale traces of its various
abilities and features (the "machinic embodiments" of nondiegetic
machine acts I discuss in chapter 1), is mostly unlinked from the
gameplay layered within it. The game, like all other digital objects, is
but a vast clustering of variables, ready to be altered and modified.
Visual design and gameplay are variables like any other. The gaming

industry has recognized this as a key characteristic of gaming. In fact, the industry's magnanimity has worked to its advantage. After the release of the source code for the successful game *Half-Life*, a group of enterprising fans of the game modified the code and released the multiplayer game mod *Counter-Strike*. The mod was so successful that Valve, the company who had originally released the code, licensed the mod, sold it commercially, and it too became commercially successful. In essence, Valve outsourced development to its fan base.

Valve benefited by cultivating the game mod community. But the reverse relationship is also crucial: game modders benefit from, and in fact require, commercial games, game engines, and hardware to make their work. Few new-media artists build their own game engines from the ground up, and practically none of them build their own computers. So, ignoring physical hardware for a moment, there exists a symbiotic relationship between mod artists and the industry in a way not seen in previous avant-garde movements. In fact, an overview of artist-made game mods reads like a laundry list of commercial game engines: *SOD (Wolfenstein 3D)*, *untitled game (Quake)*, *Adam Killer (Half-Life)*, *QQQ (Quake)*, *911 Survivor (Unreal)*, *Bio-tek Kitchen (Marathon Infinity)*, and so on. Counterexamples exist, of course, including the artist Paul Johnson, who creates his own game systems (not to mention his own hardware), or ROM hacking and classic gaming mods, whereby artists like Cory Arcangel code all their software from scratch with little reliance on any existing commercial game. Nevertheless, at the technical level there remains a close relationship between mod artists and the industry.

Having acknowledged this, I would like to continue by pointing out a series of differences between, on the one hand, the formal poetics of gaming, loosely adopted from the gaming industry, and on the other hand, the various formal conventions used in a variety of artist-made game mods. By "formal poetics of gaming," I mean the total system of gameplay experienced by the gamer. This includes the design techniques and aesthetic approaches practiced widely in the gaming industry and detailed in books like *Rules of Play*.[7] Granted, the differences between any two commercial games can be quite significant (compare, for example, *Rez* to *SSX*, or *Riven* to *Mario Kart*), while the differences between a commercial game and a mod can be as superficial as *Tomb Raider* and *Nude Raider*. So while it is clear that neither side of my albeit artificial aesthetic division is easily massed together in a single category of "commercial" versus "avant-garde," nevertheless grant me my crude classification scheme so that we may try to rummage through the various formal distinctions separating the ever-growing pile of blockbuster games churned out by the industry on the one hand and the somewhat smaller list of artist mods on the other.

A Formal Grammar

Transparency versus Foregrounding

This principle, adopted from Wollen, is particularly apt for understanding the video game avant-garde. In the cinema, this principle refers to the apparatus of filmmaking and whether or not that apparatus—microphones, lights, the film strip, the director and crew—is removed from the image, making the apparatus *transparent*, or included within the image, thereby *foregrounding* the apparatus. Hollywood almost universally removes the apparatus from the image, while art or avant-garde filmmaking is often unafraid to include it in any number of visual experiments. In gaming, this same division is evident: mainstream games almost never reveal the guts of the apparatus, while artist-made game mods do so quite often. Because the technical apparatus of gaming is quite different from film, so too the status and quality of foregrounding is different. The gaming apparatus may be foregrounded through image or through code.

An apt analogue to Godard in contemporary computer art is the European duo known as Jodi (a name formed by joining the first names of the group's two members, Joan Heemskerk and Dirk Paesmans). I have already mentioned their work in passing but have yet to examine them in any detail. The fresh, formalist radicalism of Jodi's work occupies a similar position today as Godard's films did in the sixties, albeit without his militant politics.[8] They are an excellent example of the countergaming technique of "foregrounding." Jodi works with computers in the same way that Dan Sandin works with video or Raymond Queneau worked with words—irreverently manipulating a medium at its most fundamental level. The centerpiece of their first American exhibition, "INSTALL.EXE," was % *My Desktop*, a large four-channel projection with a simple pretext: screw with the icons on a typical computer desktop so violently that they become interesting to watch. The chaotic desktop-as-medium engendered half repulsion, half rapt fascination. Florian Cramer calls their work "a clever simulation of unpredictability performed in software."[9] Jodi has made work in a variety of formats, particularly on the Internet, and they have also created a series of computer games. With the work *SOD* in 1999, Jodi established the standard for today's artist's game mod. Since then they continue to make games, crafting the ultraretro *JET SET WILLY Variations @ 1984*, and the ultramodern *untitled game*. This last work, *untitled game*, foregrounds the gaming apparatus both through the use of visual material and through code. The work often lapses into pure data, streaming real-time code up the screen with little or no representational imagery at all (see the sections "A-X," "M-W," and "V-Y"). This is a way of foregrounding the apparatus of the game's source code. But at other times, the code is ignored, and the image apparatus is foregrounded purely through the kaleidoscopic interplay of images.

The glitch effects of *r/c* or *QQQ* (nullpointer/Tom Betts) also illustrate this image-based method of foregrounding. And in still other instances, the two methods of foregrounding are mixed, as shown with Vuk Cosic's *ASCII Unreal*, which both elevates the status of pure code and projects that code into a three-dimensional visual environment, or in Lonnie Flickinger's *Pencil Whipped*, which foregrounds the constructedness of character models, levels, and sounds by crafting them anew via a low-fi cartoon aesthetic.

Gameplay versus Aestheticism

The tendency to privilege foregrounding over transparency runs in tandem with another principle of countergaming: aesthetics are elevated over gameplay. This is certainly not a necessary quality of countergaming, yet current work tends in this direction. Conventional gamic form relies on a notion of purposeful interactivity based on a coherent set of game rules. Narrative and form are smoothly joined. But countergaming often has no interactive narrative at all and little gameplay supported by few game rules, if any. In this sense, countergaming replaces play with aesthetics, or perhaps something like

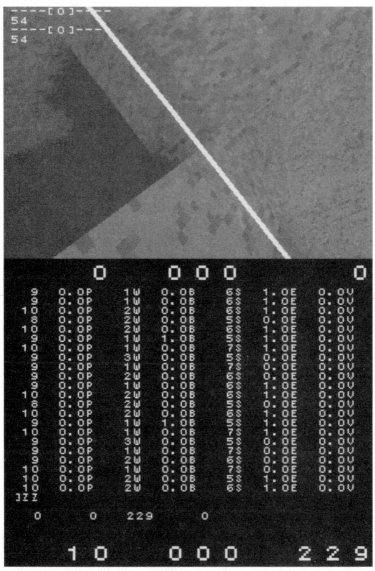

Jodi, *untitled game*, 1996–2001. Reproduced with permission of Jodi.

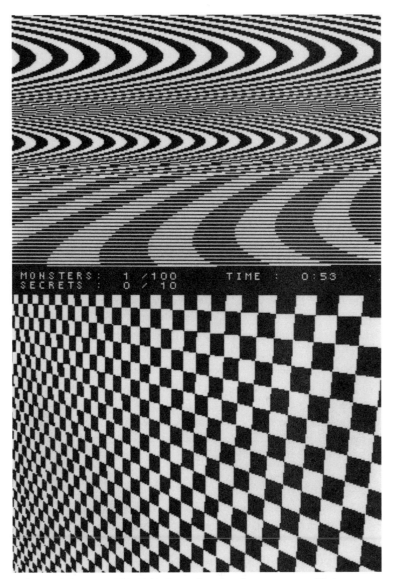

Jodi, *untitled game*, 1996–2001. Reproduced with permission of Jodi.

the play of signification. This is the same move from Caillois to Derrida described in chapter 1. A common outcome of having no gameplay is having no explicit narrative. Mods like *Adam Killer, Super
Mario Clouds* (Cory Arcangel), and most of Jodi's work follow this
tendency—Pit Schultz refers to this as "aestheticizing the technical
error."[10] In all these works, any conventional sense of gameplay is
obscured. The game engine persists (albeit often stripped down and
dissected to near death), but it is repurposed to serve the same sort of
modernist formal experiments that the avant-garde has pursued for
decades. A slightly different approach to the use of unintended narratives is seen in *Velvet Strike* (Anne-Marie Schleiner, Brody Condon, and Joan Leandre), or in Condon's in-game performance titled
Worship. While not technically mods, these works still attack conventional gamic form by creating unintended scenarios and narratives
inside the game. They create conditions of estrangement and unpleasure, to use Wollen's terminology. Consider also the example of machinima (like *Red vs. Blue* [Rooster Teeth Productions], Jim Munroe's
My Trip to Liberty City, or Eddo Stern's *Sheik Attack*) where artists
remove gameplay altogether, substituting it with the rote choreog-
raphy of a noninteractive video. All these examples show how, in
countergaming, aesthetic experimentation often trumps interactive
gameplay. Now, this doesn't seem to hinder avant-garde gaming at all.
It merely serves to focus its attention on a few key areas while excluding others. Specifically, the three aesthetic realms most often modified
in artist game mods are space, visuality, and physics. Modding the
flow of gameplay itself is less common.

Representational Modeling versus Visual Artifacts

Conventional gamic form is based on a visual principle of representational modeling. This means that volumes are constructed so that
they closely resemble the plastic shaping of real forms, be they fictional
or not. Following this approach, a well-designed game has a high
level of representational fidelity: objects in the game may be entirely
imaginary and have no real-world referent, but they must always be
cohesive and represented as objects with an actual relationship to
gameplay. Glitches in the graphics engine break the illusion of representational modeling. Eddo Stern calls these glitches "artifacts":

I am borrowing the term artifact from computer science where the term is used in reference to undesired cosmetic disturbances such as jagged edges or dirty patches in an image file (common in compressed digital video or jpeg images for example), excess noise or hiss in a sound stream, or unpredictable ASCII characters in a text file. Artifacts differ from bugs, which are usually caused by programming mistakes; artifacts don't prevent functionality per se, but cause an unperfected aesthetic disturbance.[11]

The existence of visual artifacts in a game tends to diminish the effects of representational modeling. The latter tends to cleanse the image of any problematic pixels, while the former highlights the misplaced textures, broken lighting effects, and other mistakes that might exist in a game's graphics engine. This heuristic is similar to the concept of "foregrounding" mentioned previously. However, the actual technology being foregrounded is much more subtle in the case of visual artifacts. Artifacts don't necessarily call attention to themselves as such, whereas foregrounding the gamic apparatus in the form of code can be quite surprising indeed. For example, the op art visual effects of Jodi's *SOD* or *untitled game* (particularly the sections "Ctrl-9," "Ctrl-F6," "Ctrl-Space," "O-O," "Slipgate," and "V-Y") are visual artifacts resulting from both the lack of anti-aliasing in the game's graphics engine and a baseline screen resolution of seventy-two dots per inch, but the streaming onscreen code in the work ("A-X," "M-W," and "V-Y") is a deliberate effort to foreground the real-time data of the game software. The results are similar, even if the techniques are different.

Natural Physics versus Invented Physics

Conventional gamic form tends to mimic the simple laws of Newtonian physics. Even when these laws are bent or broken in a game, the physical properties and behaviors of objects usually remain inside some type of plausible logic. Thus the "bullet time" effect in *Max Payne* or *Enter the Matrix* or *Tony Hawk's Underground 2* or any number of other games breaks Newton's laws but still follows a somewhat coherent idea of material physics. Bullet time simply slows down motion and suspends this or that object in ways that are still intelligible. *Untitled game* (particularly the sections "E1M1AP," "I-N," and "Q-L"), on the other hand, introduces a set of entirely counterintuitive

Tom Betts, QQQ, 2002. Reproduced with permission.

physical laws, wherein space warps and spins for no reason at all. The physical laws of the work are not predictable or intelligible. They are entirely invented.

The current heuristic also pertains to the physics of visuality. The glitch effect known as "trailing" (or "hall of mirrors"), where the background image is not refreshed as objects pass across it, resulting in an iterative smear effect, is often used in artist-made game mods, as in r/c, *Adam Killer*, or *QQQ*. This effect is, in essence, an invented physics of visuality. In this new optics, visual images persist and diminish in ways unfamiliar to human eyes. They linger and mix according to the artist's rules, not the rules of physiology. More to the point, they explicitly defy conventional design techniques for optics in gaming, techniques that try to mimic the visual physiology of human sight as best they can.

Interactivity versus Noncorrespondence
Conventional games privilege the faithful, one-to-one relationship between user actions on the controller and resultant actions in game-play. A jump results in a jump, a rightward motion results in a right-

Tom Betts, QQQ, 2002. Reproduced with permission.

ward motion, and so on. This player-game relationship is crucial for constructing diegetic space and creating a feeling of interactivity during gameplay. The gamer must be able to effect change in the game using the controller and see those changes instantly reflected in the game. But, to comment again on Jodi's *untitled game*, in artist mods the keyboard and mouse often become uncoupled from the physical space of the game entirely, leaving the player at a loss for any type of faithful interactivity. Anne-Marie Schleiner recounts her experience viewing the work:

> Unlike ID Software, the original designers of Quake, JODI search for beautiful bugs in the system, to make glitches happen that weren't supposed to, to tweak the game, even to demolish it. When I push the spacebar to jump in E1M1AP instead the world rotates uncontrollably. In G-R the screen refreshes non-stop with bright RGB colors, (no navigation at all). In Ctrl-9 and Ctrl-Space, navigation and looking about generate undulating black and white moire patterns. . . . In E1M1AP, when I hit the space bar to jump, I summersault into an extended disorienting twirl. Output far exceeds input. Or the program becomes the performer, I am no longer player god in control—I must concede some of my agency to the code.[12]

So while user input in mainstream gaming is matched moment by moment with a subsequent response inside the game engine, in countergaming there may not be such a one-to-one relationship, and in fact some user input may be completely ignored or interpreted in radically unexpected ways. "The moment a system crashes, the moment in which a user can no longer test the effects of his or her work, the moment control is lost and the system takes on its own materiality, all these moments are appreciated and examined in all their detail by Jodi," writes Pit Schultz.[13] (This is why, in chapter 1, I referred to Jodi in the context of nondiegetic machine acts.) Many artist game mods are completely noninteractive, not unlike watching a game play by itself in demo mode. *Super Mario Clouds* is a good example of this. Or consider Eddo Stern's *Fort Paladin: America's Army*, which celebrates the removal of interactivity entirely by robotically automating the act of gameplay. The work is less game than sculpture.

Radical Action

Some of the remaining heuristics from Wollen are less applicable for countergaming. At first glance, the "fiction versus reality" pairing appears appropriate. Mongrel's game *BlackLash* lets players fight against swastika-bearing spiders and hooded Ku Klux Klan members. Part video game, part social commentary, *BlackLash* illustrates the drama of political activism in a gaming format. "Here is your chance to kick some arse and annihilate the powers that be and smack them into the next millennium," writes Mongrel.[14] There are also other mods and conversions that deal with social reality: *The Great Game* by John Klima; Natalie Bookchin's *AgoraXchange* design initiative; *Antiwargame* by Josh On/Futurefarmers; *Escape from Woomera*, staged in the Woomera immigration detention camp in Australia; *911 Survivor*, a restaging of the World Trade Center attacks of 2001; and C-level's *Endgames: Waco Resurrection*, which reworks David Koresh's 1993 last stand at the Branch Davidian compound—the game is based, they write, on "alternative utopias and apocalyptic moments." These are all artist-made games that reject traditional notions of fictional narrative in favor of real-life scenarios (and, interestingly enough, these are not mods per se but entirely new games unto themselves). Yet the conceit of real-life simulation has been a staple of

Josh On/Futurefarmers, *Antiwargame*, 2002. Reproduced with permission.

commercial gaming since Ralph Baer modeled tennis, hockey, and skiing in the early 1970s.

Today games like *Gran Turismo, The Getaway,* or *True Crime* are based on real-world maps with high degrees of verisimilitude. So gaming's use of reality is entirely different from Godard's use of reality. It doesn't have the same political import, a subject I explore in chapter 3. Further, the privileged status of reality in both film and television has changed greatly since Godard's heyday, moving into the mainstream with reality television programming like *Survivor* or (pseudo)reality filmmaking like *The Blair Witch Project.* So perhaps "fiction versus reality" is not a useful classification scheme for gaming (or cinema anymore, for that matter). Likewise, Wollen's first pairing, "narrative transitivity versus narrative intransitivity," also appears inappropriate for video gaming, owing to the necessarily open-ended structure of most gamic narrative.

Mainstream games like *Tony Hawk's Pro Skater* or *Grand Theft Auto* or *Ultima Online* succeed partly on the strength of their huge, unobstructed narrative spaces. In fact, the very concept of play precludes

Anne-Marie Schleiner, Brody Condon, and Joan Leandre, *Velvet Strike*, 2002. Reproduced with permission.

"one thing following another" in any strict, linear fashion. Instead, these games thrive on repetition, rewinding and backtracking, story-on-a-rail episodic structures, digressions into minigames, and other nonlinear techniques. Finally one is prompted also to scrap Wollen's "single diegesis versus multiple diegesis." Games greatly complicate the concept of diegesis. As I suggest in chapter 1, the nondiegetic in gaming is often on equal footing with the diegetic, whereas in classical narrative cinema the nondiegetic is rarely foregrounded as such. Thus games constantly "rupture between different codes and different channels," to use Wollen's words, transitioning fluidly from the (mostly) nondiegetic HUD to diegetic weapons, or from configuration menus to normal gameplay.

Here is a summary, then, of the formal differences between conventional video gaming and countergaming:

1. *Transparency versus foregrounding.* (Removing the apparatus from the image versus pure interplay of graphics apparatus or code displayed without representational imagery.)

2. *Gameplay versus aestheticism.* (Narrative gameplay based on a coherent rule set versus modernist formal experiments.)
3. *Representational modeling versus visual artifacts.* (Mimetic modeling of objects versus glitches and other unexpected products of the graphics engine.)
4. *Natural physics versus invented physics.* (Newtonian laws of motion, ray tracing, collisions, etc., versus incoherent physical laws and relationships.)
5. *Interactivity versus noncorrespondence.* (Instant, predictable linkage between controller input and gameplay versus barriers between controller input and gameplay.)

Looking at this list, one may conclude that there exists no true avant-garde of gamic action today. In other words, countergaming is essentially progressive in visual form but reactionary in actional form. It serves to hinder gameplay, not advance it. It eclipses the game as a game and rewrites it as a sort of primitive animation lacking any of the virtues of game design. This is essentially the reason why Jodi's work is apolitical, while Godard's was hyperpolitical: Jodi aims to create better abstraction, not to create better (or different) gameplay. We need an avant-garde of video gaming not just in visual form but also in actional form. We need radical gameplay, not just radical graphics. So here is another principle, which I hope will further develop the as yet unrealized potential of art gaming:

6. *Gamic action versus radical action.* (Conventional gaming poetics versus alternative modes of gameplay.)

By radical action, I mean a critique of gameplay itself. Visual imagery is not what makes video games special. Any game mod focusing primarily on tweaking the visual components of a game is missing the point, at least as far as gaming is concerned. Artists should create new grammars of action, not simply new grammars of visuality. They should create alternative algorithms. They should reinvent the architectural flow of play and the game's position in the world, not just its maps and characters. Ruth Catlow's *Activate: 3 Player Chess* does this; the Etoy *Toywar* did this; the "everybody must win" philosophy of Fuller's "World Game" also shows the way—an evocative idea when one considers that these works exhibit almost none of the given countergaming principles. Other examples are few and far between.

So countergaming is an unrealized project. An independent gaming movement has yet to flourish, something that comes as no surprise, since it took decades for one to appear in the cinema. But when it does, there will appear a whole language of play, radical and new, that will transform the countergaming movement, just as Godard did to the cinema, or Deleuze did to philosophy, or Duchamp did to the art object. And more importantly, artist-made game mods will be able to resolve the essential contradiction of their existence thus far: that they have sought largely to remove their own gameplay and lapse back to other media entirely (animation, video, painting). This will be a realization of countergaming *as* gaming, just as Godard was a realization of countercinema *as* cinema. The New Wave was new once, and so were new media, but as Godard wrote in 1965, after having made a half dozen of his best films, "I await the end of Cinema with optimism." The countergaming movement should aspire to a similar goal, redefining play itself and thereby realizing its true potential as a political and cultural avant-garde.

Notes

1. Gamic Action, Four Moments

1. I use the term "video game" with some inaccuracy. To be precise, a video game refers to a game played on a console using a video monitor. In such a specific definition, the term would exclude arcade games, games played on personal computers, those played on mobile devices, and so on. It is for simplicity's sake that I use "video game" in its colloquial sense as an umbrella term for all sorts of interactive electronic games.

2. Some suggest, and I partially agree, that "player" is a better overall term than "operator." My goal in avoiding the term "player" is not to eliminate the importance of play, as will be evident later, but instead, by using "operator," to underscore the machinic, almost industrial, and certainly cybernetic aspect of much of human-computer interaction, of which gaming is a key part. Additionally, "operator" tames, if only slightly, the anthropomorphic myth of the distinctly and uniquely human gamer, and that can only be a good thing in my mind. Operators are, in a majority of instances, organic human players, but they may also be any type of intelligent play agent such as a bot or script. Hence the greater neutrality of the term "operator" appears fitting. Readers who are resistant should mentally cut and paste "player" for "operator" in the present chapter; the switch is entirely tolerable.

3. Espen Aarseth, "Computer Game Studies, Year One," *Game Studies* 1, no. 1 (July 2001). Aarseth uses the term "ergodic" to describe action in

media. See Aarseth, *Cybertext: Perspectives on Ergodic Literature* (Baltimore: Johns Hopkins University Press, 1997).

4. I have never been happy with the word "interactivity." "I find the concept to be too broad to be truly useful," Lev Manovich writes. Because it is too broad, the concept is not included as a central principle of new media by Manovich. Most so-called old media are also interactive, he goes on to claim: "All classical, and even moreso modern, art is 'interactive' in a number of ways. Ellipses in literary narration, missing details of objects in visual art, and other representational 'shortcuts' require the user to fill in missing information." See Manovich, *The Language of New Media* (Cambridge: MIT Press, 2001), 55–56. This echoes what Umberto Eco calls the lazy machine: "Every text, after all, is a lazy machine asking the reader to do some of its work." See Eco, *Six Walks in the Fictional Woods* (Cambridge: Harvard University Press, 1995), 3. It is my contention, though, that traditional "texts" are not machines at all, at least not in the way that a computer is a machine. Thus I make a distinction between those art forms that require the physical action of both the user and the work for the work to exist, and those that do not. In the end, of course, such distinctions are largely strategic, aiming to elevate a new medium by laying claim to some space of aesthetic specificity, a pursuit repeated over and over in the various avant-gardes and artistic zigzags of the modern era.

5. See Philip Agre, "Surveillance and Capture," in *The New Media Reader*, ed. Noah Wardrip-Fruin and Nick Montfort (Cambridge: MIT Press, 2003).

6. Roger Caillois, *Man, Play and Games*, trans. Meyer Barash (New York: Schocken Books, 1979), 10.

7. Johan Huizinga, *Homo Ludens: A Study of the Play-Element in Culture* (Boston: Beacon, 1950), 13.

8. Gérard Genette uses "extradiegetic" (instead of "nondiegetic") to designate the narrating instance itself, as opposed to the actual narration: "*Any event a narrative recounts is at a diegetic level immediately higher than the level at which the narrating act producing this narrative is placed.* M. de Renoncourt's writing of his fictive *Mémoires* is a (literary) act carried out at a first level, which we will call *extradiegetic*; the events told in those *Mémoires* (including Des Grieux's narrating act) are inside this first narrative, so we will describe them as *diegetic,* or *intradiegetic*." See Genette, *Narrative Discourse: An Essay in Method* (Ithaca, N.Y.: Cornell University Press, 1980), 228.

The question of narrative is somewhat controversial in game studies: the narratologists claim that video games are simply interactive narratives, while the ludologists claim that games must be defined separately from the concept of narrative. At the end of the day, I side with the ludologists, but I find that the diegetic-nondiegetic split, despite being rooted in a theory of narrative, is still useful for understanding the different types of gamic action. For a good analysis of how narrative fits into gameplay, see Katie Salen and Eric Zimmerman, chapter 26 of *Rules of Play* (Cambridge: MIT Press, 2004), 377–419.

9. My distinction here is similar to the one made by Nick Montfort in his analysis of interactive fiction. His "commands" are my diegetic operator acts; "directives" are nondiegetic operator acts; "replies" are diegetic machine acts; and "reports" are nondiegetic machine acts. See Montfort, *Twisty Little Passages: An Approach to Interactive Fiction* (Cambridge: MIT Press, 2003), 25–28.

10. This phrase was suggested by Katie Salen.

11. James Newman, "The Myth of the Ergodic Videogame: Some Thoughts on Player-Character Relationships in Videogames," *Game Studies* 2, no. 1 (July 2002).

12. The purest form of this is probably found in Maurice Blondel, *Action (1893): Essay on a Critique of Life and a Science of Practice* (Notre Dame: University of Notre Dame Press, 1984). James Somerville's *Total Commitment: Blondel's "L'Action"* (Washington, D.C.: Corpus, 1968) is a useful secondary source on Blondel's text. Blondel's interest is the irreducibility of action. Today the word "interactive" is often invoked to describe the coupling of user and machine, but Blondel's concept of action is more singular, more oriented around the individual life, or what he called the whole of man. "Yes or no, does human life make sense, and does man have a destiny?"—this query begins what is perhaps the most extensive and uncompromising consideration of action in the history of philosophy. "It is into action that we shall have to transport the center of philosophy" is his premise, "because there is also to be found the center of life" (3, 13). And so I take Blondel as inspiration, but not for the motivations of action, and not the consequences of action, nor the moral foundations of this or that action. Those related debates in the analytic philosophy tradition try to derail a study of pure action by reducing it to other topics, as if a study of causes and effects could shed any light on the actual phenomenon of doing. Blondel's book aims to answer, not unlike Descartes, a foundational question for human destiny. "In my acts," he wrote, "in the world, inside of me, outside of me, I know not where or what, *there is something*" (52). Indeed, the same theme has reoccurred often in philosophy, from Epicurus's "swerve" of atoms as they fall through space to Deleuze and Guattari's "refrain" abetting the forces of chaos.

13. Clifford Geertz, *The Interpretation of Cultures* (New York: Basic Books, 1973), 10.

14. Ibid., 436. The seeming irrationality of "deep play" in cockfighting goes against the source of the expression, which is found in Jeremy Bentham: "Take away from a man the fourth part of his fortune, and you take away the fourth part of his happiness, and so on. . . . It is to this head that the evils

of deep play ought to be referred. Though the chances, so far as relates to money, are equal, in regard to pleasure, they are always unfavourable. I have a thousand pounds. The stake is five hundred. If I lose, my fortune is diminished one-half; if I gain, it is increased only by a third. Suppose the stake to be a thousand pounds. If I gain, my happiness is not doubled with my fortune; if I lose, my happiness is destroyed; I am reduced to indigence." See Bentham, *Theory of Legislation* (London: Trubner, 1871), 106.

15. Geertz, *The Interpretation of Cultures*, 444.

16. Ibid., 446.

17. Gregory Bateson, "A Theory of Play and Fantasy," in *Steps to an Ecology of Mind* (Chicago: University of Chicago Press, 1972), 180.

18. Indeed, for Schiller the play-drive is synonymous with man's moral freedom and his aesthetic experience. See, in particular, letters 14 and 15 of Friedrich Schiller, *On the Aesthetic Education of Man* (Oxford: Oxford University Press, 1967).

19. Huizinga, *Homo Ludens*, 28. A slightly more detailed summary of the concept appears earlier in the book: "Summing up the formal characteristics of play we might call it a free activity standing quite consciously outside 'ordinary' life as being 'not serious,' but at the same time absorbing the player intensely and utterly. It is an activity connected with no material interest, and no profit can be gained by it. It proceeds within its own proper boundaries of time and space according to fixed rules and in an orderly manner. It promotes the formation of social groupings which tend to surround themselves with secrecy and to stress their difference from the common world by disguise or other means" (13).

20. Caillois, *Man, Play and Games*, 43. A more verbose definition appears on pages 9–10.

21. Huizinga, *Homo Ludens*, 173, 46.

22. "All these [objectionable] hypotheses have one thing in common: they all start from the assumption that play must serve something which is *not* play." Huizinga, *Homo Ludens*, 2.

23. Caillois, *Man, Play and Games*, 10, 11.

24. Vilém Flusser, in a nod to Huizinga's own simple periodization from *Homo sapiens* to *Homo faber* to *Homo ludens*, underscores the eventual transformation of play into algorithmic terms by using the word "program": "The new human being is not a man of action anymore but a player: *homo ludens* as opposed to *homo faber*. Life is no longer a drama for him but a performance. It is no longer a question of action but of sensation. The new human being does not wish to do or to have but to experience. He wishes to experience, to know and, above all, to enjoy. As he is no longer concerned with things, he has no problems. Instead, he has programs." Flusser, *The Shape of Things* (London: Reaktion, 1999), 89.

25. Huizinga, *Homo Ludens*, 14–15.
26. Jacques Derrida, *Writing and Difference* (Chicago: University of Chicago Press, 1978), 280, 278, 281, 292. The French *jeu* is translated as either "play" or "game," or, as one might say today, "gaming."
27. Jacques Derrida, *Dissemination* (Chicago: University of Chicago Press, 1981), 194, 95.
28. Derrida, *Writing and Difference*, 289 (translation modified by the author).
29. "If one takes the line of thought that runs from Heraclitus via Nietzsche to Deleuze and Derrida," McKenzie Wark writes, "one might rather say that play is a free movement that can engender more rigid structures. It is not the game that is the precondition of play, in other words, but play that is the condition of possibility of the game. Brian Massumi argues this most cogently in his book *Parables of the Virtual*." See Wark, "Designer Playtime," *Rhizome Digest*, January 5, 2004.
30. Salen and Zimmerman, *Rules of Play*, 305.
31. Derrida, *Writing and Difference*, 292 (translation modified by the author).
32. Derrida, *Dissemination*, 156–57.
33. Huizinga, *Homo Ludens*, 10.
34. Eddo Stern, "A Touch of Medieval: Narrative, Magic and Computer Technology in Massively Multiplayer Computer Role-Playing Games," http://www.eddostern.com/texts/Stern_TOME.html (accessed April 25, 2005).
35. This same machinic logic of image making is evoked in John Simon's 1997 Internet artwork *Every Icon*. The work draws every image that is combinatorially possible within a 32 × 32 pixel square by sequentially turning on and off pixels. In essence, the work is binary mathematics turned into image.
36. Remedy, "Part III, Prologue," *Max Payne* (New York: Rockstar Games, 2001) (italics mine).

2. Origins of the First-Person Shooter

1. Michel Foucault, "Of Other Spaces," *Diacritics* 16, no. 1 (Spring 1986): 25.
2. See Lev Manovich, "The Automation of Sight: From Photography to Computer Vision," in *Electronic Culture* (New York: Aperture, 1996), 229–39.
3. See Paul Willemen, *Looks and Frictions* (Indianapolis: Indiana University Press, 1994).
4. For more on this type of look, see Marc Vernet, "The Look at the Camera," *Cinema Journal* 28, no. 2 (Winter 1989): 48–63.
5. Fredric Jameson, *Signatures of the Visible* (New York: Routledge, 1992), 112.

6. David Bordwell, Janet Staiger, and Kristin Thompson, *The Classical Hollywood Cinema* (New York: Columbia University Press, 1985), 31–32.

7. For discussion of subjective and POV shots in early cinema, see Bordwell et al., *The Classical Hollywood Cinema*, 32–33. J. P. Telotte notes the use of subjective shot effects before *Lady in the Lake* in the 1944 film *Murder, My Sweet*, as well as Orson Welles's unrealized prewar plan to film *Hearts of Darkness* in a subjective camera. See Telotte, *Voices in the Dark: The Narrative Patterns of Film Noir* (Urbana: University of Illinois Press, 1989), 104.

8. Bonitzer continues: "There is a misinterpretation [in the film] which fails to understand that it is not at the place of the subject that the camera operates, but at the place of the Other." Bonitzer, "Partial Vision: Film and the Labyrinth," *Wide Angle* 4, no. 4 (1981): 58.

9. J. P. Telotte, "The Detective as Dreamer: The Case of *The Lady in the Lake*," *Journal of Popular Film and Television* 12, no. 1 (Spring 1984): 13.

10. Edward Branigan, *Point of View in the Cinema* (New York: Mouton, 1984), 80. For an altogether different approach to the subjective idiom in filmmaking, see Bruce Kawin, *Mindscreen: Bergman, Godard, and First-Person Film* (Princeton: Princeton University Press, 1978). For a discussion of these issues in the documentary film, see Barry Grant, "Point of View and Spectator Position in Wiseman's *Primate* and *Meat*," *Wide Angle* 13, no. 2 (April 1999): 56–67.

11. A much deeper discussion of dream sequences should, ideally, be included in this section. For more on this area, see R. T. Eberwein, "The Filmic Dream and Point of View," *Literature/Film Quarterly* 8, no. 3 (1980). I avoid analyzing these types of scenes primarily because dream sequences, while often employing the subjective camera, generally remain in an extra-diegetic, imaginary narrative zone within the mind of the character. Dream sequences are indeed subjective, but they are not actual and therefore are not constrained by the same formal logic as are other types of scenes. The reader should, for the time being, bundle dream sequences under my heading "Mental Affect."

12. Carol J. Clover, "The Eye of Horror," in *Viewing Positions: Ways of Seeing Film*, ed. Linda Williams (New Brunswick: Rutgers University Press, 1995), 193.

13. See, for example, R. Barton Palmer, "The Metafictional Hitchcock: The Experience of Viewing and the Viewing of Experience in *Rear Window* and *Psycho*," *Cinema Journal* 25, no. 2 (Winter 1986): 4–19.

14. Cited in Gerald Peary, "Cinema Verity: *Elephant* and *Shattered Glass* Focus on the Truth," http://www.bostonphoenix.com/boston/movies/film/documents/03313411.asp (acccessed April 15, 2005).

15. Steven Shaviro, "Regimes of Vision: Kathryn Bigelow, *Strange Days*," *Polygraph* 13 (2001): 62.

16. Vivian Sobchack, "The Scene of the Screen: Envisioning Cinematic and Electronic 'Presence,'" in *Electronic Media and Technoculture*, ed. John Caldwell (New Brunswick: Rutgers University Press, 2000), 151.

17. Jay Bolter and Richard Grusin, *Remediation* (Cambridge: MIT Press, 1999), 97.

18. Fredric Jameson, "The Iconographies of Cyberspace," *Polygraph* 13 (2001): 126.

19. Stern, "A Touch of Medieval."

3. Social Realism

1. See Patrick Crogan, "The Experience of Information in Computer Games," http://hypertext.rmit.edu.au/dac/papers/Crogan.pdf (accessed April 15, 2005), for more on the intersection of gaming and the military information society. Julian Stallabrass's early essay "Just Gaming" is also methodologically instructive for how to think about games as allegories. See Stallabrass, "Just Gaming: Allegory and Economy in Computer Games," *New Left Review* 198 (March 1993). See also Anne-Marie Schleiner's essay "Velvet-Strike: War Times and Reality Games," http://www.opensorcery.net/aboutvs.html (accessed April 15, 2005).

2. Because cinema has the image as its central material form, it follows that representation would be the primary problematic around which many debates turn, with the politically progressive solutions of, on the one hand, realism with its removal of the apparatus or, on the other, countercinema with its revelation of the apparatus. But being based on actions rather than images, games quite naturally would turn around a different problematic, something like message sending or "correspondences" where the core issue is not about mimesis or realistic depiction but about the fidelity of action to image, of motion to outcome.

3. See Huizinga, *Homo Ludens*, 15. The citation is incorporated by Huizinga from Jane Harrison, *Themis: A Study of the Social Origins of Greek Religion* (Cambridge: The University Press, 1912), 125.

4. Bruce Shelley, "Guidelines for Developing Successful Games," *Gamasutra*, August 15, 2001.

5. Jameson, *Signatures of the Visible*, 158.

6. André Bazin, *What Is Cinema?* vol. 2 (Berkeley: University of California Press, 1971), 27 (italics mine).

7. Jameson, *Signatures of the Visible*, 169.

8. Bruno Reichlin, "Figures of Neorealism in Italian Architecture (Part 1)," *Grey Room*, no. 5 (Fall 2001): 80.

9. See also Shuen-shing Lee's "'I Lose, Therefore I Think': A Search for

Contemplation amid Wars of Push-Button Glare," *Game Studies* 3, no. 2 (December 2003).

10. Donna Haraway, *Simians, Cyborgs, and Women* (New York: Routledge, 1991), 161.

11. For more on *Toywar*, see Adam Wishart and Regula Bochsler, *Leaving Reality Behind: Etoy vs EToys.com and Other Battles to Control Cyberspace* (New York: Ecco, 2003). The global nature of *Toywar* is interesting to compare to Buckmister Fuller's "World Game," mentioned in chapter 4. Fuller's game is a very early example of a global asset management simulation game.

12. I first learned of *Special Force* through a March 2003 e-mail post to *Rhizome Raw* from Jennifer and Kevin McCoy. *Under Ash* is being followed by another, similar game called *Under Siege*.

4. Allegories of Control

1. On this point, Markku Eskelinen writes: "Historically speaking this is a bit like the 1910s in film studies; there were attractions, practices and very little understanding of what was actually going on, not to mention lots of money to be made and lost." See Eskelinen, "The Gaming Situation," *Game Studies* 1, no. 1 (July 2001).

2. See Philippe Sollers, "Programme," *Tel Quel*, no. 31 (Fall 1967): 3–7, (italics mine); and Roland Barthes, "La mort de l'auteur," in *Le bruissement de la langue* (Paris: Éditions du Seuil, 1984), 66 (italics mine).

3. Fredric Jameson, *Postmodernism, or The Cultural Logic of Late Capitalism* (Durham: Duke University Press, 1991), 168 (italics mine).

4. The editors of *Cahiers du cinéma*, "John Ford's *Young Mr. Lincoln*," in *Movies and Methods*, ed. Bill Nichols (Berkeley: University of California Press, 1976), 496.

5. Fredric Jameson, *The Political Unconscious* (Ithaca, N.Y.: Cornell University Press, 1982), 291–92.

6. Gilles Deleuze, *Negotiations* (New York: Columbia University Press, 1995), 178.

7. Gilles Deleuze, "Having an Idea in Cinema," in *Deleuze and Guattari: New Mappings in Politics, Philosophy and Culture*, ed. Eleanor Kaufman and Kevin Jon Heller (Minneapolis: University of Minnesota Press, 1998), 18 (translation modified by the author).

8. Branden Hookway, *Pandemonium: The Rise of Predatory Locales in the Postwar World* (New York: Princeton Architectural Press, 1999), 23–24.

9. Ted Friedman, "*Civilization* and Its Discontents: Simulation, Subjectivity, and Space," http://www.duke.edu/~tlove/civ.htm (accessed August 14, 2003). I will use *Civilization* to refer to the entire game series. When talking about a particular installment in the series, I will specify, as in *Civilization III*.

10. Manovich, *The Language of New Media*, 222.

11. R. Buckminster Fuller, *Your Private Sky: The Art of Design Science* (Baden, Switzerland: Lars Müller Publishers, 1999), 473, 479. For more on the globalistic and synergistic philosophy of the World Design Initiative, see also Fuller, *Your Private Sky: Discourse* (Baden, Switzerland: Lars Müller Publishers, 2001), 247–78.

12. Caillois, *Man, Play and Games*, 4.

13. See Salen and Zimmerman, *Rules of Play*, 515–34; and Brian Sutton-Smith, *The Ambiguity of Play* (Cambridge: Harvard University Press, 2001).

14. Friedman, "*Civilization* and Its Discontents."

15. Pete Loshin, *Big Book of FYI RFCs* (San Francisco: Morgan Kaufmann, 2000), xiv.

16. For a technical overview of network protocols, see Eric Hall, *Internet Core Protocols: The Definitive Guide* (Sebastopol, Calif.: O'Reilly, 2000); or for a more interpretive approach, see my book *Protocol: How Control Exists after Decentralization* (Cambridge: MIT Press, 2004).

17. Jonathan Postel, "Transmission Control Protocol," RFC 793 (September 1981), http://www.faqs.org/rfcs/rfc793.html (accessed April 15, 2005).

18. Lisa Nakamura, *Cybertypes: Race, Ethnicity, and Identity on the Internet* (New York: Routledge, 2002), 114.

19. Theodor Adorno, *Aesthetic Theory* (Minneapolis: University of Minnesota Press, 1998), 317. See also Stallabrass's essay "Just Gaming," a brilliant critique of play no doubt inspired by Adorno's commentary on Schiller and Huizinga.

20. Fletcher gives a succinct etymology of the term: "*Allegory* from *allos* + *agoreuein* (other + speak openly, speak in the assembly or market). *Agoreuein* connotes public, open, declarative speech. This sense is inverted by the prefix *allos*. Thus allegory is often called 'inversion.'" See Angus Fletcher, *Allegory: The Theory of a Symbolic Mode* (Ithaca, N.Y.: Cornell University Press, 1964), 2.

21. Blondel, *Action (1893)*, 207.

22. Bateson, "A Theory of Play and Fantasy," 180.

5. Countergaming

1. Game mods have been exhibited in a fine art context for several years. See particularly "Cracking the Maze" (online, 1999); "Game Show" at MASS MoCA (2002); "Killer Instinct" at the New Museum of Contemporary Art in New York (2003); and "Games: Computergames by Artists" in Dortmund, Germany (2003).

2. Katie Salen, personal correspondence, September 27, 2004.

3. Tilman Baumgärtel, "Games-Modifications by Artists," *Nettime*, October 27, 2003.

4. Peter Wollen, *Readings and Writings: Semiotic Counter-Strategies* (London: Verso, 1982), 80–81.

5. Ibid., 80–89.

6. Anne-Marie Schleiner, "Parasitic Interventions: Game Patches and Hacker Art," http://www.opensorcery.net/patchnew.html (accessed April 15, 2005).

7. See Salen and Zimmerman, *Rules of Play*, an invaluable resource on game design.

8. While Jodi's work is devoid of political messages, the creators do exhibit a blanket political disgust toward all things commercial or mainstream, as a famous incident in California illustrates, recounted here by Josephine Bosma: "When [Jodi] received the 'Webby Award,' a kind of Internet-Oscar, in the category 'Art' in 1999, they stayed true to their bad reputation: During the ceremony in San Francisco, the acceptance speech of every winner must not contain more than five words. Jodi addressed the audience that consisted mainly of new-economy-people with: 'Ugly-commercial-sons-of-bitches.'" See Bosma, "Jodi and the Cargo Cult," in the exhibition catalog *INSTALL.EXE–JODI* (Basel: Christoph Merian Verlag, 2002), 95.

9. Florian Cramer, "Discordia Concors: www.jodi.org," in *INSTALL.EXE–JODI*, 71.

10. Pit Schultz, "Jodi as Software Culture," in *INSTALL.EXE–JODI*, 84.

11. Stern, "A Touch of Medieval."

12. Anne-Marie Schleiner, "2 Reviews—*Untitled Game* and *Ego Image Shooter*," *Rhizome*, March 12, 2002.

13. Schultz, "Jodi as Software Culture," 83–84.

14. See http://www.mongrel.org.uk/Natural/BlackLash (accessed April 15, 2005).

Index

Alexander R. Galloway is assistant professor in the Department of Culture and Communication at New York University.